Quick Guide to Winter Herbs & Christmas Spices – Ancient Healing Wisdom & Modern Use

Cold Season Herbal Gardening, Spice & Herbal Recipes for Wellness & Health, Images to Color

Written by Carol Roy
Published by LEAFinPRINT

www.leafinprint.com

Contents

Recipes

Every herb and spice presented comes with recipes, tricks and tips on how to use them. Below a list of the recipes shown.

ABBREVIATIONS:

Tbsp = tablespoon
Tsp = teaspoon
Vegetarian and vegan menus are included.
Low heat = 120-150°F/48-65°C
Medium heat = 250-304°F/121-162°C

STRESS RESILIENCE WORKBOOK WITH SEASONAL HEALING HERBAL INFUSIONS

16 Tools for Balanced Health & Focused Energy through Nutrition Matching your Body Type & Mindfulness Practice

Breathe a stress-free life. This book is full of actionable advice to help you balance your seasonal body reactions, break the stress cycle, and achieve true positivity. - The keys lie within yourself – understanding your body's natural rhythms and learning to work with them.

https://www.leafinprint.com/books

HERBALIST'S GUIDE TO NATIVE AMERICAN REMEIDES

From the same publisher

Medicinal Plants and Herbs, Powerful Herbal Traditions and Remedies for your Effective Home Apothecary Table

Introduction

We celebrate Christmas deep in the darkest middle of winter, close to the winter solstice, at a time when our freezing ancestors cuddled up to fires, sheltering from storms. Nowadays, we gather with family and friends in heated homes. Festive food for this season always uses spices, bringing warmth to the food and drink, as well as to the hands holding hot cups, appealing to the tongue, the nose, and the eye. Whereas herbs are commonly grown in the country where they are used, spices originate abroad bringing a scent of the exotic to our Christmas drinks, savory food, and desserts.

In the first part of this book we will examine 8 winter spices. In the second part, we have chosen 10 herbs. In both parts, we first look at the history and traditions of the winter months and Christmas, through both its herbs and spices. Then we focus on the plant description, healing properties and ancient and medicinal use of each plant. We conclude with how the spices are used in the kitchen, for beverages, spices that work well together in cooking, with recipes, tricks and tips on how to use them.

The second part of this book includes instructions on how you can grow herbs outdoors and indoors for winter use. This will allow you to harvest herbs throughout the cold winter and enjoy the health benefits fresh herbs can bring to your winter diet.

In summary, each **Spice and Herb** chapter contains information about:

1. History, Legends & Modern Times
2. Healing Properties and Ancient and Modern Medicinal Use
3. Recipes, Tricks & Tips using the Spice or Herb
4. How to grow chosen herbs indoors or outdoors.

For more details, please consult the reference section at the end of the book.

But for now, let's dive into the magic world of herbs and spices!

Precautions Using Herbs and Spices

Cooks have been using herbs and spices for centuries in the kitchen to add a spicy flavor to gingerbread cookies, Christmas beverages, and puddings. This cookbook offers you many ways to utilize herbs and spices in your kitchen. Adding them to your food will give you all their health benefits as well as their taste.

Less well-known to the modern western world is how widely they are used as herbal medicine, and as a natural alternative to prescription drugs worldwide. 80% of the world's global population uses herbal preparations regularly. Although herbs and spices are natural, it is still important to view them as drugs with possible side effects, if taken incorrectly.

When using herbal medicine for the first time, some people report feeling under the weather and assume the herb is not working. However, to the trained herbalist this is a sign that the opposite is actually true. Your body is releasing toxins and your symptoms are the result. Continue the whole treatment (even if you are skeptical) as this allows the herb to work as planned.

Use the right herb or spice for the proper condition. Never think that an herb used to treat sciatica like chamomile or lavender will also improve a headache. Drink plenty of water; the effects of herbal medicine are subtle and they utilize water to dilute and release toxins or to balance vital systems. As our bodies are 75% water, the herb can dilute any toxin and then release it. Water allows the herbal medicine to create movement and tiny changes to achieve the desired result.

If you start adding more herbs and spices into your daily consumption and feel unwanted side effects, see a trained herbalist, and take their advice. It is important to use the dosage prescribed and to notice any changes in your body like feeling tired, thirsty, or flu-like symptoms. Chat with your herbalist if in doubt. A good herbalist will warn you of possible symptoms in advance.

If you are pregnant or take any medication, inform your practitioner who can advise of spices and herbs that are safe for you.

PRECAUTIONS USING HERBS AND SPICES

The Antioxidant and Anti-Inflammatory Properties of Herbs and Spices

Since the 1990s the antioxidant properties of foods have been promoted and used as a marketing tool for foods and supplements. But what are antioxidants and why are they good for us?

Free radicals are generated naturally in our body as food is turned into energy, as well as after exercising or exposure to cigarette smoke, air pollution, and even sunlight. The cells of our bodies are constantly affected by free radicals that can damage them. This can increase the risk of chronic, oxidative stress-related diseases like cancer or cardiovascular disease.

Vitamins, and other natural antioxidants, can be added to our diet to help. There are hundreds, maybe thousands of different substances that can act as antioxidants. The most familiar ones are vitamins C and E, beta-carotene, and other related carotenoids, along with the minerals selenium and manganese. Studies show that foods containing antioxidants tend to work best in combination with other nutrients, plant chemicals, and even other antioxidants.

All the spices presented in this book and some of the herbs are packed with antioxidants, and many are also said to have excellent anti-inflammatory properties.

It should be noted that research is ongoing, and it will take time to test and identify all the health benefits of spices. However, as spices have been used throughout history for taste and health, I recommend adding more to your diet and observing how they are affecting you. As you taste your Christmas mulled wine, or hot chocolate with added spice goodness, I am confident you will not only enjoy the taste but also feel the warmth and goodness spreading right through you.

For people wanting to acquire more in-depth knowledge on that subject, please consult the references in the resources at the end of this book.

THE ANTIOXIDANT AND ANTI-INFLAMMATORY
PROPERTIES OF HERBS AND SPICES

Winter and Christmas Spices

Why do we associate Christmas with these winter spices?

The essence of a Christmas spice is that it warms the soul, as well as our senses. Although today, we can buyspices easily, they do not actually grow here. In fact, there is a long religious and economic history of their availability in our stores. International trade routes were fought over historically because spices were precious and only used by the wealthy, seen as a status symbol.

Nowadays, Christmas is a time when people give themselves a treat using these spices while also enjoying their warming benefits in the winter. The spices presented here were chosen for their popularity in the Western World but many more could be added to the list.

It may surprise you that in hotter climates, spices doubled up as preservatives to keep food fresh. Cinnamon, for example, used in cooking from India through Indochina and the Caribbean, has been shown to inhibit the growth of the bacterium E.Coli, keeping food both tasty and fresh. Ginger is used in many Asian countries to keep the common cold at bay.

Buying and Storing Spices

Spices from abroad can often be bought in your supermarket or local Asian and Indian markets or from online suppliers. There are some savings to be made by ordering in bulk if you have a group of family members or a community group. However, the fresher the better when it comes to herbs and spices, so that only amounts that can be consumed within the year or so should be purchased. Spices can arrive whole and dried, (like cloves and cardamoms) or ground into powder (like allspice) or both, in stick form and powder form, like cinnamon.

Check the spices if you buy them fresh; they should smell magnificent. With ginger, check that the root is not shriveled because this means it is stale. Star Anise should have no broken parts so turn over the spice with a spoon to check it is complete.

You can mill your own spice, for instance from Star Anise or make herb oil, if you have dried cinnamon bark, bay, or fresh lavender and rosemary. Traditionally, they have been ground with a mortar or pestle, which is in itself a meditative process and enjoyable because you gradually become aware of the scent of the spices. However, this is a time-consuming process so you can also buy a spice grinder to speed up the process.

To store spices, you will need airtight containers and make sure they are not in direct sunlight to conserve their quality for as long as possible. All ground spices lose some of their strength over time so if you cannot smell them, they may have lost their freshness. Sometimes you can fry the spice lightly in oil in a pan to test it, and if it still smells good, then use the spice as soon as you can. I would not keep most spice for much more than a year.

Anise or Star Anise, *verum*

History, Legends & Modern Times

Most people describe the smell of Star Anise as sweet. Its distinctive, aniseed flavor comes from the dried fruit of an evergreen tree native to China and Indonesia.

Its arrival in Europe came via the tea route from China and since the 1500s, the pods and star-shaped fruit have been used in syrups and desserts. Also known as Chinese Star Anise, Star of Anise, or Badiana, its star shape certainly suits the Christmas theme of this book. Its fragrant oil is a familiar scent to most of us in skin cosmetics, perfume, and cooking, not to mention the alcoholic liqueurs such as Galliano, Sambuca, and Pastis.

In the kitchen, you can add the star or pods to soups and casseroles and remove them before serving. You can grind both the pods and stars into powder but note that this will degrade quickly so use it soon after grinding. If you tie some red or green string around a few of these and hang them as alternative Christmas decorations on your tree or in strategic places around your house, then Star Anise will certainly bring the scent of Christmas into your home in a very subtle way.

Healing Properties and Ancient and Modern Medicinal Use

Star Anise seeds are traditionally offered after meals to aid digestion, decrease bloating and relieve nausea. Many mothers will recognize it as a natural treatment for colic in babies. The sweet, aniseed scent of Star Anise is also utilized in aromatherapy, cosmetics, soaps and to disguise unpleasant scents of other pharmaceuticals.

The aromatic oil has been shown to contain vitamins A and C, and thymol, which has become a useful spice for treating influenza, coughs, and respiratory infections.

The seed pods of Star Anise or the star are used in cooking. These are collected from the tree before they are fully ripe and then dried in the sun. A native of Indonesia and China, it has a close relative in the Japanese Star Anise, but these seed pods are poisonous if consumed. They are commonly used as incense but make sure for *consumption* that you purchase Star Anise (*Illicium verum*).

Recipes, Tricks & Tips Using Anise

Anise is primarily used as a Christmas spice for cookies, gingerbread, honey cake, and punch.

Anise also refines vegetables such as red cabbage, carrots, meat and fish dishes.

Anise harmonizes with other spices such as caraway, cardamom, nutmeg, cloves, pepper, star anise, and cinnamon. In addition, interesting flavors are obtained when anise is combined with chocolate or orange.

Aniseed is used to flavor several liqueurs and spirits. The most well-known are Arak (from Lebanon, 50 – 54% alc.), Raki (from Turkey, ~45% alc.), Ouzo (from Greece, 37.5–45% alc.), and Pastis (from France, ~45% alc.). The alcohol is gained mainly from grapes or today from sugar cane or wheat alcohol and fruits. Anise is used for flavoring, and in the case of Ouzo and Pastis, other spices are added, like cardamom, clove, coriander, fennel, and nutmeg, among others.

5-Spice Pork Tenderloin with Star Anise

In this recipe, we take inspiration for a 5-spice marinade to apply before you cook your pork dish. Three star Anise shapes can be added to the dish to serve, but too much can be overpowering, so it's best to add these at the end of the cooking process.

Serves: 4
Prep time: 50 minutes
Cook time: 2 hours

Make the Marinade and Pork Tenderloin

Ingredients

- 5 Spice is a Chinese spice mixture containing ground star anise, cinnamon, cloves, fennel, and peppercorns.
- 18 oz (500 g) pork tenderloin
- Salt to rub on the meat and to taste
- 2 Tbsp of olive oil
- 5 Spice mix
- 3 apples
- 2 onions

Method

1. Use 1 tsp of each of the 5 Spice ingredients and pulverize them in a mortar or a food processor (see the recipe section of Coriander to learn more about this process).

2. For cooking the pork tenderloin, first, rub both sides with salt to slightly dry the meat. This allows the meat to absorb the spices.
3. Then, brush olive oil all over the pork. Rub the 5 Spice mixture into both sides of the pork, and cover with foil to marinate overnight.
4. Preheat the oven to 390°F (200°C).
5. Add 1 Tbsp of oil to the base of a heavy baking dish and place the pork inside.
6. De-core 3 apples and slice them to fit underneath the pork. Cooking juices will fall onto the apples directly, and the juices can be collected at the end of cooking to make gravy.
7. Peel and chop 2 onions and cut these into quarters to place on both sides of the pork.
8. Allow the meat to cook for 35-40 minutes. Check if the pork is cooked by placing a skewer in the meat to check if the juices run clear, not red.
9. After the meat is ready, remove the dish from the oven and carefully remove some juices. Then place the dish back in the oven and allow a further 10 minutes to crisp the edges of the meat.
10. Remove the meat to a wire tray or serving dish, and then use the juices to make a sauce by adding 1 teaspoon of flour to thicken and a little water. Stir well and use this to pour over the meat when served on the plate.
11. To serve, decorate with 3-star Anise shapes on the meat before carving.
12. Serve with roast potatoes and vegetables, and carve slices of meat for each person.

Allspice, *Pimenta Dioica*

History, Legends & Modern Times

Allspice is the name for the ground, unripe berries of the Myrtle tree *Pimenta Dioica*. This spice was known to have been used for embalming by the Maya and the Aztecs in Mexico, at the time of the Conquest of Central America by the Europeans. In 1494, explorers unpacked the unripe berries in the UK, who believed it was a type of pepper and gave it the Latin name *pimento*.

In the US, it was named allspice and ground into a fine powder which is the flavor of mulled wine or New England mulled cider. These perfect drinks for the festive season are packed with cloves, allspice, cinnamon, and nutmeg.

Native to Jamaica, Mexico, and the West Indies, this is the spice used in Jerk Chicken and it is very popular in the Middle East cooked with lamb or used to flavor hummus. Allspice is one of the 4 spices used in Pumpkin Pie spice which also contains nutmeg, cinnamon, and ginger. At Christmas and during winter, allspice adds its unique taste in the kitchen to both sweet and savory dishes.

Healing Properties and Ancient and Modern Medicinal Use

Allspice grows in warm, tropical regions worldwide. The flower buds form in bunches and are picked before they are fully ripe. These buds resemble pepper seeds when dried. In addition to being used for cooking, the berries of allspice are also used to make medicine. They contain both Eugenol and Gallic acid as well as glycosides and polyphenols with analgesic and anti-neuralgic actions in painful conditions. Therefore, it has been used to ease heavy monthly bleeding in menstrual cycles.

Traditionally, it was used rubbed directly on painful or a bloated stomach to ease indigestion or gas.

The Eugenol contained in the spice made from the berries is widely used in dentist's surgeries as a method of killing germs. For this, it is used orally as a mouthwash, and is added to toothpaste as a flavor. The spice is often rubbed directly on sore gums to soothe toothache.

Allspice leaves are known as a natural pesticide in the countries where it grows. Recent medical trials on cancer cells have shown that allspice from the berries may have anti-tumor abilities.

Recipes, Tricks & Tips Using Allspice

Allspice can be used in various sweet and savory dishes, including cookies, spice cake, sausage seasoning, pumpkin pie, and ham glazes.

It's a crucial component of Jamaican Jerk seasoning, a fiery concoction of herbs and spices that instantly transform chicken or pork into a party.

Allspice is one of the 4 spices used in pumpkin pie spice, which also contains nutmeg, cinnamon, and ginger.

Pumpkin Pie using Allspice

Here is a creamy sweet and spicy pumpkin pie you can serve as easily on Christmas as on Thanksgiving Day. The seeds can be toasted after the pie is cooked for snacks.

Serves: 2
Prep time: 10 minutes
Cook time: 70 minutes

Ingredients

- 1 pumpkin, 35 oz/1 kg
- 2 tsp allspice
- 1 cinnamon stick *optional*
- Freshly grated nutmeg
- 1 Tbsp brown sugar
- 1.7 oz/50 g raisins or sultanas
- 75 ml rum
- 10.58 oz/300 g sweet pastry dough
- 2.64 oz/75 g caster sugar

- 2 eggs
- 1 lemon, juiced and zest
- 1 orange, juiced and zest
- 1.76 fluid oz/50 ml cream

To decorate: Icing sugar

Method

1. Preheat the oven to 375°F/190°C.
2. Place raisins in a bowl and marinate them with the rum while the pumpkin cooks.
3. Cut the pumpkin through the center first, separate it into slices and remove the seeds (for roasting). Place the slices onto a baking tray and add a few pinches of allspice, some fresh ground nutmeg, and the brown sugar evenly over the slices.
4. Cook for 40-45 mins until the flesh is soft. Then reduce the heat to 325°F/160°C.
5. In a saucepan, add the raisins and the rum and cook gently. Do not boil, or the alcohol will evaporate. The raisins should look plump by now and absorb a lot of the rum, already adding flavor to the pie.
6. Time to bake the pie crust! Roll out the dough to slightly less than half an inch deep (4 mm). Butter an 8-inch sponge or quiche pan and then carefully line it with the bottom of the dough. Allow the dough to overhang at the edges. Now it's time to bake the crust by itself. You will add the filling later, once cooked.

7. Bake for about 15 minutes. You can trim the edges to make them look neat. Turn up the oven to 350°F/180°C, and let's make the filling.
8. Now pulse the cooked pumpkin flesh with the juice of both orange and lemon, the caster sugar, and the remaining zest of the fruit.
9. Add the strained raisins and a pinch of allspice or nutmeg. Beat in the eggs and cream, stirring to a smooth consistency.
10. Pour the filling into the pie crust until it reaches the top. If using cinnamon sticks, break them into smaller pieces and sink them into the pie filling. It will need to be baked for 30 minutes, and then remove it from the oven and allow it to cool while you eat dinner.
11. Use the warm oven to toast your pumpkin seeds for snacks.
12. To serve, use the icing sugar to create a snowy effect on the top of the tart and serve with ice cream.

mortar and pestle (left), spice grinder (right)

Cardamom, *Elettaria cardamomum*

History, Legends & Modern Times

Cardamom has been used by humanity for over 4000 years. It was used in Egypt both as an aromatic oil and a spice. It was also involved in the process of embalming the dead for their journey to the afterworld. It is believed that the Vikings also discovered cardamom on their sea voyages, and so it was introduced to Scandinavia between the eighth and eleventh centuries. Modern use in Scandinavia includes cardamom flavoring for mulled wine, as a winter warmer.

In southern India, the spice plant grows freely in an area called Cardamom Hill. Nowadays, India, Guatemala, and Nepal vie to be the largest exporter. There is some variety in the size of seed available with India producing smaller pods and Guatemalan pods being slightly larger. In cooking across the world, cardamom is a favorite flavor for curry dishes while in Asia, cardamom tea is offered as a drink.

Osiris, ancient Egypt's god of the underworld. According to the myth, Osiris was a king of Egypt who was murdered and dismembered by his brother Seth. His wife, Isis, reassembled his body and resurrected him, allowing them to conceive a son, the god Horus. He was represented as a mummified king, wearing wrappings that left only the green skin of his hands and face exposed. (www.britannica.com/)

Healing Properties and Ancient and Modern Medicinal Use

Indian Ayurvedic medicine recommends cardamom for indigestion, asthma, and bad breath. In Asia, the seeds are chewed after meals to increase oral hygiene and freshness. Traditionally, cardamom is used to de-stress people, causing relaxation and aiding digestion, thereby leading to a good night's sleep. Cardamom tea is often drunk in Asia and consumed to reduce symptoms of the common cold.

However, cardamom is not completely absorbed by the human digestive system.

Be particularly wary of chewing cardamom seeds and digesting them if you have trouble with gallstones or are susceptible to them. Overconsumption of this spice may eventually cause gallstones if you are susceptible.

There may also be some interactions with antidepressants, anticoagulants, and HIV medication. Therefore, before using this spice as a medicine, please speak to an herbalist or medical practitioner to ask them about possible interactions.

Recipes, Tricks & Tips Using Cardamom

Cardamom adds the perfect kick to any meal, whether sweet or savory. The "Queen of Spices," or green cardamoms, are among the most expensive spices, surpassed only by vanilla and saffron.

Do you know the difference between "Turkish Coffee" and "Arab Coffee?" In both cases, the strong brew is made with finely ground coffee and served with the grounds in small porcelain cups. In the picture below, the cup is protected by a decorative metal holding. However, cardamom is added during the brewing process in Israel and other parts of the Middle East but not in Turkey. This style of coffee preparation is linked to the tradition of fortune-telling by interpreting the grounds of the coffee after you finish drinking the liquid.

Cardamom adds a special something to cocktails, and the pods look decorative floating in the drink.

Cardamom Onion Soup

After the excesses of Christmas day, this soup is a tasty, light lunch you can top with grated cheese and serve with toast. Don't forget to remove the cardamom pods and bay leaf before you serve.

For a vegetarian recipe, substitute the chicken stock with vegetable stock.

Serves: 2-4
Prep: 15 minutes
Cook: 30 minutes

Ingredients

- 4 large onions
- 3 cloves of garlic
- Salt and black pepper to season
- 1 bay leaf
- 1 tsp cardamom pods
- 1 tsp of turmeric
- 1 tsp of cumin
- 1 cup (250 ml) chicken stock
- 3/4 cup (180 ml) white wine
- 2.5 cups (600 ml) water to cover the onions

To serve: Grated cheese and toast

Method

1. Peel and chop onions into similar-sized pieces that will cook evenly.
2. Add the olive oil to the saucepan with a pinch of salt and black pepper.
3. Add the bay leaf, cardamom pods, cumin, and turmeric, and stir the spices to ensure they cook well in the oil for 5 minutes. Turn the heat to medium (120-150°F/48-65°C). Cooking the spices will infuse the dish and allow the cardamom to scent the onions.

4. Add the onions and fry for 5 minutes until they are golden brown.
5. Next, add the chicken stock and the whole peeled garlic cloves to the pan to cook slowly for 15 minutes until soft. Then, bring to a boil to cook the garlic thoroughly, as it will eventually dissolve into the soup.
6. You can add a little extra water to feed more people!
7. Allow simmering for another 10 mins, stirring occasionally.
8. I like the chunky texture of the soup, but if you prefer a smoother consistency, you can place it in a food processor to make a thick, tasty soup.
9. To serve, pour into bowls but remove the bay leaf and cardamom pods. Top with grated cheese and serve with warm toast.

 WINTER AND CHRISTMAS SPICES

Cinnamon, *Cinnamomum verum, (Also known as Cinnamomum zeylanicum)*

History, Legends & Modern Times

Our festive mince pies are packed with spices and we eat them with little knowledge of their origin. The original mincemeat pies were cooked in the Middle East and eaten by the Crusaders, in their battles to free the Holy Lands from Seljuk Turks. These pies were filled with meat and dried fruit, soaked in alcohol and spices, including cinnamon, cloves, nutmeg, and pepper. The knowledge of spices grown in this area became common in Europe and as these plants were not native to Europe, the lucrative spice journeys were undertaken by sea and on arduous land trips.

Cinnamon is little known as a preservative but modern laboratory tests show that it can reduce and inhibit the bacteria Listeria and *E.Coli.* Using it in cooking helped our ancestors to preserve their food for longer.

When Christopher Columbus originally sailed from Portugal in 1492 to discover a new sea route to Asia, it was in hope that he could locate lands where valuable spices grew. He believed for some time after landing in the Americas, that he had sailed around the world to the East. Nowadays it is hard for us to understand but at that time the form of the earth was still unknown, therefore no international maps appeared on seafaring navigation tools, let alone on mobile phones! The spices grew in far-off lands, and he discovered America but not the spice route.

In medieval times, a spiced wine flavored with cinnamon called Hippocras, (or *Hypocras)*, was a treat enjoyed in France during the festive season and widely adopted by other countries during the winter holidays. Perhaps this is the direct origin of mulled wine that features so widely in Christmas markets from Scandinavia to Germany and has become the tradition we know and love so well in the States.

For our festive preparations, we buy cinnamon bark or ground cinnamon as a spice, using it in drinks and baking. A sprinkling of cinnamon on a hot chocolate or a cinnamon bark addition to a cocktail really says winter is here.

Healing Properties and Ancient and Modern Medicinal Use

There are various trees from which a type of cinnamon (or cassia) can be cut. The true cinnamon tree is *Cinnamomum verum* and to obtain cinnamon, the bark has to be cut or peeled and then dried in the sun, when it usually curls into the shape we buy our cinnamon in shops. These can be later ground into powder. The trees grow in China, Vietnam, and Indonesia.

Cinnamomum aromaticum (also known as *Cinnamomum cassia*) is often used as a substitute for *Cinnamomum verum*. The ground cinnamon bought in our shops may actually be a mixture of the two cinnamon types. Cassia bark has a flavor that is similar to but less aromatic than cinnamon and the buds of Chinese Cassia are sold as cassia buds. The bark tends to be thicker than *Cinnamomum verum*.

Traditional medicine in Asia often advises cinnamon use for digestive problems, for irritable bowel syndrome, and as a supplement for diabetes. There are some concerns about the overuse of cinnamon in pregnancy or the use of cassia

Cinnamomum verum or True cinnamon, Cinnamon stalk with flowers and bud

for patients with any kind of liver disorder, so please consult an herbalist and discuss if it is suitable for you to use it for medical purposes.

Recipes, Tricks & Tips Using Cinnamon

For me, this spice says Christmas like no other. Cinnamon is an essential ingredient for mulled wine (see nutmeg for the recipe).

On Christmas day, if you make fresh mince pies, this is an activity that can be shared by everybody in the family!

Adding a stick of cinnamon to hot chocolate or a cocktail will allow the spice to infuse any drink. You can also grate fresh cinnamon onto custards and cookies to give them an extra special sweet spice taste.

Make cinnamon syrup. Just pop 2-3 sticks into a pan of boiling water and allow the cinnamon to infuse for 5 minutes. Add 3 teaspoons of sugar and cloves, if you like, and stir well until the sugar has dissolved. Allow it to cool and then store it in the fridge to add to non-alcoholic drinks for children or cocktails for their parents.

Mince Pies using Cinnamon

A tip is to make your "mince" beforehand and have it ready in your fridge. This will save time on Christmas day. The fruit soaks up the flavor of the brandy, so your mince pies will have the sweetness of cinnamon and the warmth of the brandy infused into the fruit.

Serves: 12
Prep time: Mince 40 minutes / Pies: 30 minutes
Cook time: 30-35 minutes

Make the Mince Filling

Ingredients

- 9 oz (250 g) raisins
- 9 oz (250 g) currants
- 1 large apple, skinned and cut into small pieces
- Enough brandy to cover the fruit
- 1 tsp cinnamon, cloves, and nutmeg
- 7 oz (200 g) sugar
- 10.5 oz (300 g) suet
- 2 satsumas, peeled and in segments

Method

1. Put the sugar in a sterilized container.
2. Then add all the other ingredients to the jar and top it up with brandy.
3. Add 1 tsp cinnamon and any other spice you wish. You will need approximately 9 oz (250 g) of the

mixture to make 12 pies, which will yield 2 sets of pies.

4. Leave to infuse for up to 2 weeks before Christmas and shake it every few days to ensure the spices mix throughout the mixture.

Make the pastry

This is a very relaxing part of the festive season for me. I like to make breadcrumbs myself. If time is short, just put all the ingredients into a food processor.

Ingredients

- 2.1 oz/60 g butter
- 3.5 oz/100 g plain flour
- A pinch of salt
- 1 egg yolk
- A little beaten egg for glazing the pies
- A little milk (optional) or water if required.

Method

1. Cut the butter into smaller pieces and allow it to go soft.
2. Put the butter in a baking bowl and add the salt.
3. Start adding the flour gradually while you mix in the egg yolk with your fingers until you have a soft pastry dough.
4. It's best to put this into the fridge to cool for at least an hour, and then you can roll the pastry dough on a flat surface. This is a favorite activity

for grandchildren or children; they can each fill their own mince pie once it's done.

5. Make 12 circles using a circular cutter and place these in the muffin pan (cupcake) baking tray as the base of the pie.

6. Fill each pie with a small amount of mince. Do not be tempted to overfill them because suet is known for oozing out while cooking.

7. Cut out 12 more circles that will go on top of the filling and secure them by pinching them together at the edges. Children can add an initial, too, if they want to recognize their pie.

8. Glaze each pie with the beaten egg using a spoon or pastry brush for a shiny finish.

9. Cook for 25-35 minutes at 350°F (175°C) or until golden brown on top. Check after 25 minutes that they are not burning. Serve when they have slightly cooled to avoid burning small mouths!

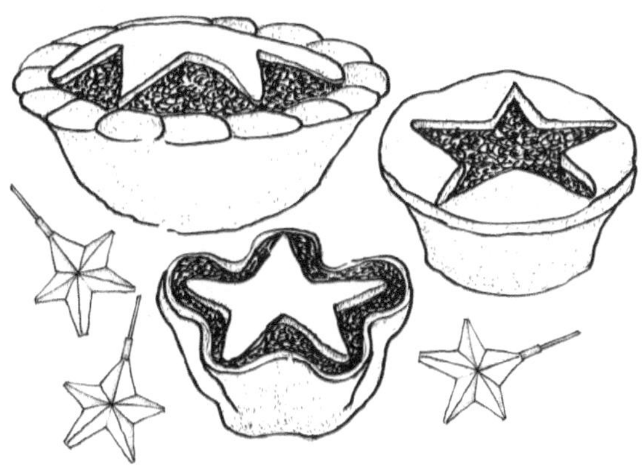

Mince pies with Cinnamon, Anise, and Cloves

Cloves, *Syzgium aromaticum*

History, Legends & Modern Times

Mainly grown in Indonesia and the Spice Islands but also in China, cloves first arrived in Europe during the Middle Ages. These are the spices that were delicately placed in orange pomanders, a circular holder for an orange studded with cloves. These decorative holders originally were placed in the rooms of patients recovering from long-term illnesses to scent the room pleasantly, but they quickly became part of the cold weather and Christmas traditions in Europe.

Dried clove buds were valued in India for cooking and are known in China since at least the 3rd century BCE (the Chinese Han period) where these dried clove buds were known as "chicken tongue spice". Chickens cannot detect spice on their tongues, so they were able to eat food with cloves without problems, even if it was deemed too spicy for humans. Spicy food rejected by humans was often given as leftovers for the chickens.

In Indonesia, planting a clove tree was traditional for the birth of a new child and as its typical lifespan was up to 80 years, the tree could live as long as the child for whom it was sown. The scent of this spice and its flowers is very fragrant and its use in remedies for colds in Europe and the US is common with honey and lemon and cloves added to keep the symptoms at bay.

Today in India and Nepal masala chai tea is often offered to guests, with cloves added.

Healing Properties and Ancient and Modern Medicinal Use

Dried cloves are the buds of the flowers of the clove tree, and are picked just before the flower opens, which can be seen in the central, round bud in the dried clove. Clove trees grow in the North Moluccan islands in Indonesia and China. Cloves are said to need to be close to the coast as they enjoy sandy, warm coastal soil and conditions. Clove oil has been used as a way to soothe the gums or to ease toothache, by spreading it topically on the area.

The oil is antiseptic and numbs and calms the area to which it is applied.

Before toothpaste was common, cloves were also chewed to freshen the breath, an ancient tradition in China, when it was recommended before an official meeting!

Nowadays, cloves are known to contain eugenol, which helps to reduce inflammation, so adding cloves to your diet may help in conditions such as arthritis or swelling. Cloves contain vitamins A, and K, manganese, potassium, and also beta-carotene, which is an antioxidant.

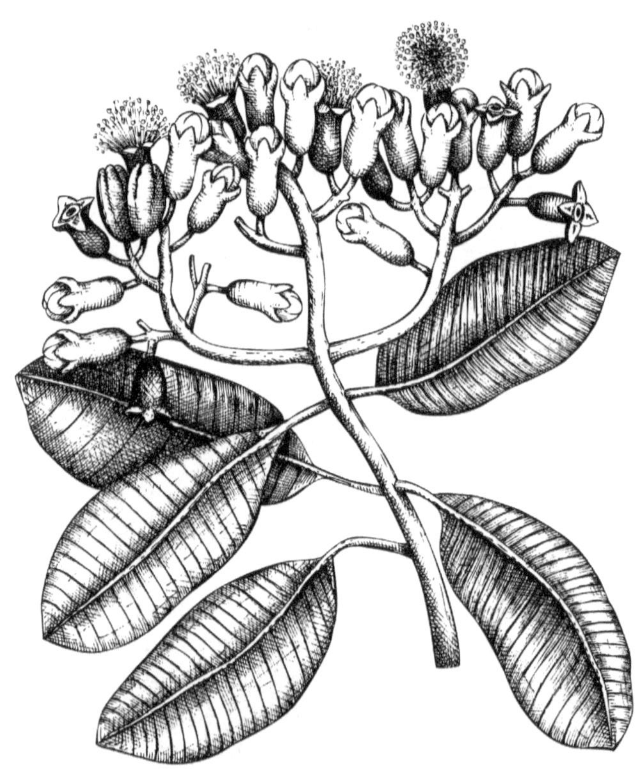

Recipes, Tricks & Tips Using Cloves

Cloves are often used in remedies for colds in the U.S., with honey and lemon added to tea for example, to keep the symptoms at bay. In India, masala chai tea with cloves is often offered to guests.

Make your own Christmas pomander (air freshener) in early December by tying a colored ribbon around an orange. Secure with a pin or a sewing stitch and a loop at the top to hang it. Then, make tiny holes in the orange peel and stick cloves in the holes. You will enjoy the gorgeous scent that fills the room you place it in.

Apple Crumble with Cloves

This recipe is a way to use extra apples on hand, as they will be cut up and cooked inside a pie. The topping was traditionally made from leftover crumbs, but you can also use plain flour. This recipe can be adapted with different fruit, but cloves may not suit all fruit. Cherries pair with cinnamon or nutmeg, for example, but hot cloves and apples are just perfect.

Serves: 8
Prep Time: 30 minutes
Cook Time: 30 minutes

Make the Crumble

Ingredients

- 3.5 oz /100 g plain flour
- 3.5 oz/100 g butter
- 4.4 oz/125 g caster sugar
- A pinch of salt

Method

1. Cut the butter into smaller cubes and let it come to room temperature.
4. Sieve flour and sugar into a bowl and add the butter cubes. Add a pinch of salt.
5. Wash your hands well, and then use your fingers to blend the flour and butter.
6. Set the mixture aside and make the apple filling.

Apple Filling

Ingredients

- 2 lb/900 g apples
- 4.4 oz/125 g granulated sugar (You can reduce this if you don't want too much sugar or use a sweetener here).
- 1 tsp ground cloves or ½ tsp whole cloves (However, people really don't like picking out cloves from desserts!)
- ¼ tsp ground nutmeg (optional)

Method

1. Preheat the oven to 425°F (220°C)
2. Peel the apples and slice them into medium-sized pieces. Do not use cooking apples – you want something sweet and juicy for this dessert. Put them in a baking bowl.
3. Shake the cloves (and nutmeg, if using) and sugar directly onto the apples. Mix with a wooden spoon and allow the mixture to sit for 10 minutes.
4. Add the mixture to a greased baking dish and add the crumble topping. Bake for 25–30 minutes or until golden brown.
5. Serve straight from the oven in bowls with cream, ice cream, custard, or nothing. There are many approaches to the correct topping for apple crumble, and an ongoing online discussion between the U.S. and Europe. You decide!

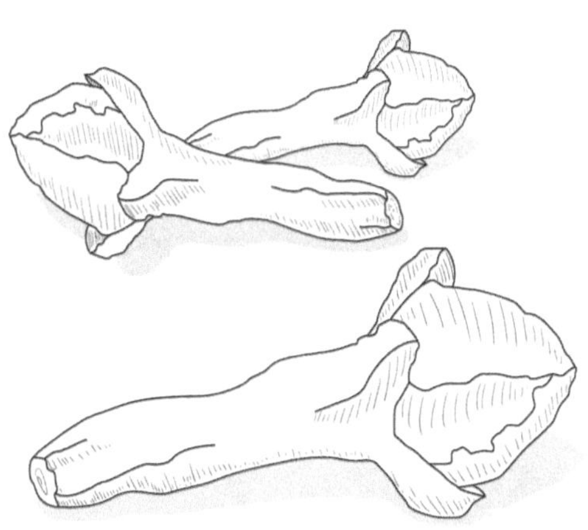

Coriander seed, *Coriandrum sativum*

History, Legends & Modern Times

Coriander leaves are known as cilantro in the US and its seed is coriander, whereas, in Europe, both the seed and the leaf are known as coriander. Native to Italy originally, it is cultivated all over the world from the Mediterranean including Egypt and Morocco, to China, India, and sub-Saharan Africa.

Coriander seeds can be used added to soups and casseroles and removed before serving but they can also be ground into powder. It should be used shortly after as the powder tends to lose its flavor quite quickly. If in doubt, smell it and if you cannot smell that sweetness, add some freshly ground spice and toast it all together for a few minutes in a hot pan.

Coriander plant with flowers, leaves, and seeds

Coriander is often used in cosmetics. After milling it, you will recognize its pleasing soft fragrance in soaps and creams. The sweet taste of coriander is often used to disguise the unpleasant taste of some prescription medicine.

Healing Properties and Ancient and Modern Medicinal Use

Traditionally, coriander seed has been recommended for good digestion and flatulence in India and other parts of Asia, and by many traditional medicines. Sometimes constipation can be alleviated by using this seed regularly. Coriander seed tests have shown that coriander extract has improved the body's tolerance and utilization of glucose, which is associated with diabetes treatment. It is wise to discuss this with your specialist and herbalist before starting any treatment.

Both leaves (cilantro) and coriander seeds contain vitamin K, which aids the body to allow the blood to clot and to build and repair bones. There is some evidence that LDL and HDL cholesterol levels are lowered when consuming coriander seeds regularly which contributes to keeping a healthy heart. However, a healthy diet and exercise are equally important, and not just the consumption of coriander seeds!

In Asia, coriander seed was also traditionally used as an aphrodisiac.

Be advised that if you already have low blood pressure (or take medication to reduce it) taking coriander is not advised. Also, if you are about to undergo surgery, it is best to avoid coriander for a few weeks.

Recipes, Tricks & Tips Using Coriander

Coriander seeds will impart gorgeous flavors by cooking slowly in soups, stews, pickles, and casseroles. They are frequently used in Indian dal and lentil dishes.

The ground spice from these seeds is used when you want a marinade, drink, or sauce to have a smooth consistency and taste.

You can grate fresh coriander from the seeds whenever you like but use up the powder within a day, or the flavor evaporates. It's also delicious when grated directly onto fresh custard dishes to add sweetness to the dish.

Many recipes include coriander seeds ground with ginger and cumin, particularly in Asian cooking.

You can grow fresh cilantro from the seeds - just place the seeds in a tiny pot with soil, and you can have fresh leaves as well as coriander seeds.

Make non-alcoholic drinks with cooked coriander that you pour into a jar to store like syrup. For children, this is a great way to join the adults. Add it to fruit juice like apple or pineapple and serve with a glace (maraschino) cherry and a straw to make it look festive.

Vegetarian Curry Mix with Coriander.

You can double up quantities and make enough for 2 dishes, but the flavor of coriander seeds evaporates rapidly, so I prefer to make this sauce fresh every time. The powder can be used in any recipe that needs curry seasoning.

Serves: 4
Prep time: 10 minutes
Cook time: Depends on your recipe

Ingredients

- 1 teaspoon of coriander seeds
- 1 teaspoon of cumin seeds
- 4 cloves
- 1-inch piece of fresh ginger root
- Optional: ½ tsp fresh peppercorn seeds

Method

1. Remove the skin from the ginger and cut it into smaller pieces. You may process them in a food processor, a grater, or a mortar and pestle.
2. Spice grinding methods:
3. Place the ingredients into a food processor until you have a powdery mixture.

4. Alternatively, you can grind the spices manually with a mortar and pestle. If using this method, make sure to grind in batches by placing small quantities at the bottom of your pestle and tapping them gently with the mortar. Once all seeds are cracked, it's time to grind the pieces to the bottom of the mortar until they are pulverized.
5. You can also use a coffee grinder for grinding your spices but be aware that the coffee scent may remain in the grinder.
6. Use this immediately in any recipe requiring curry sauce.

WINTER AND CHRISTMAS SPICES

Nutmeg, *Myristica fragrans*

History, Legends & Modern Times

This sweet-smelling spice was used as incense by the ancient Romans to sanctify sacred places and give their homes its characteristic scent. It was popular in Europe in the Middle Ages, and when The Ottoman Empire decided to ban trade routes via the land route from Constantinople (the old name for the city of Istanbul) in the late 15th century, nutmeg became even more valuable.

By the 1600s, it had become an important spice controlled exclusively by the Dutch, and the native location of the tree was kept secret by the original traders. European nations were battling the spice-producing countries for rights in the so-called Spice Wars. The scarcity of the spice caused great demand and high prices.

Nutmeg was presumed to be a nut when first found by Europeans and the name sticks even to the present day. However, traders found the so-called "nut" growing on ships and they realized that this was actually the seed of the tree. Sailors used to coat them with lime to stop them to germinate while on long sea journeys from source to export location.

Know that all nuts are seeds but not all seeds are nuts. A nut has a shell or harder outer casing which is removed to show the seed inside but not all seeds need a nutshell around them.

Healing Properties and Ancient and Modern Medicinal Use

A native of the Spice Islands, in Indonesia and nowadays grown in the West Indies and also in China, a nutmeg tree can produce about 15,000 "nuts" in a season. The nuts (which are actually seeds) can be ground into the powder we know as nutmeg that is added to drinks, cakes and desserts so common at Christmas. The outside tendrils of the seed are ground to become the spice we know as mace.

One caution is that the oil in nutmeg "nuts" (myristicin) can cause dehydration if taken in small amounts. Larger amounts (2-3 full nuts) cause hallucinations, nausea, and in some, palpitations as documented by Charlie Parker, the musician. However, there is no danger to anyone grinding a small portion of the nut for flavoring since large quantities of nuts would need to be consumed for any such effect.

Recipes, Tricks & Tips Using Nutmeg

Nutmeg and mace can be used for same purposes. However, mace has a more pungent, intense taste than nutmeg and is generally more expensive.

Grated nutmeg on mashed potatoes. I must admit that this is a recipe borrowed from a Turkish friend. She loves to grate fresh nutmeg on mashed potatoes and then stir this in well. Add it gradually because the taste can be overpowering if you add too much. Try 3 gratings and stir, then taste and do one more grating if you want it a bit spicier. Children love it! You can also grate fresh nutmeg onto crêpes or pancakes to add a spicy sweetness.

Mulled Wine

Serves: 4
Prep time: 10 minutes
Cook time: 25 minutes

Ingredients

- 750 ml (75 cl, 1 bottle) red wine
- 2 clementines or oranges
- 3.5 oz /100 g of caster sugar
- 1 Tbsp honey, optional
- 12 gratings of fresh nutmeg
- 1 cinnamon stick

- 4 cloves
- 1.4 cup (60 ml) brandy

To serve: 4 heat-proof glasses or cups. Fruit and spices to decorate

Method

1. Peel the clementines/oranges into segments and remove any rinds.
2. In a large saucepan on medium heat, add sugar, orange segments, and 3 oz/100 ml wine to cover the other ingredients to make a syrup.
3. After 15 minutes, check that the sugar is completely dissolved. Now it's time to infuse the spices.
4. Add 1 cinnamon stick, nutmeg, and cloves to the syrup mixture and stir well. I like to add honey at this stage for a really sweet flavor, but if you prefer your mulled wine to be drier, then do not add this.
5. Top up the saucepan with the rest of the red wine but remember that the alcohol evaporates at high temperatures, so reduce the heat to low and simmer the spices and wine for another 5-10 minutes.
6. Add the brandy just before serving and get the decorations ready. You can add 1 star anise per jar or a cinnamon stick, plus a segment of orange. Cheers!

   WINTER AND CHRISTMAS SPICES

Ginger, *Zingiber officinale*

History, Legends & Modern Times

The use of root ginger has been valued as an aid to medicine as well as a culinary delight for many centuries. Native to Asia (e.g. India, China) it was unknown in Europe until ships sailed to Asia in search of spices, and ginger became a firm favorite in the Middle Ages.

Its warmth on the tongue was noted by physicians and reports of its use as medicine came from sailors who had visited China and India. This is the spice of gingerbread, that cookie that has inspired cooks and writers! Its hot spicy goodness can be added to hot drinks as remedies for colds and flu and is often mixed with cloves and honey. It suits savory dishes in the kitchen as well as sweet and is an ingredient in many Indian and other Asian dishes.

The root of the ginger plant contains the magic, and where it grows natively in Asia, a small piece of root is dug up whenever it is needed, which enables the plant to keep growing. In fact, you may notice a green stem emerging from ginger purchased in a store, which tells you it has been out of the ground for some time.

Traditionally, gingerbread biscuits have become synonymous with Christmas, and ginger beer is another taste favored by many generations in the Western World.

Believe it or not, the ancient Greeks are reputed to have eaten small pieces of ginger with bread, as a way to settle the stomach after a large meal, which may have been the idea of the chef who developed gingerbread.

Wild ginger (*Asarum canadense*) grows throughout the eastern United States and southeastern Canada, as well as parts of Asia. It is a popular plant harvested by foragers. Despite its name, it bears no relation as it is in a completely different plant family than culinary ginger (*Zingiber officinale*). However, it is named 'wild ginger' because of the similar taste and smell of the roots. Native Americans used the root to flavor foods like we use culinary ginger today.

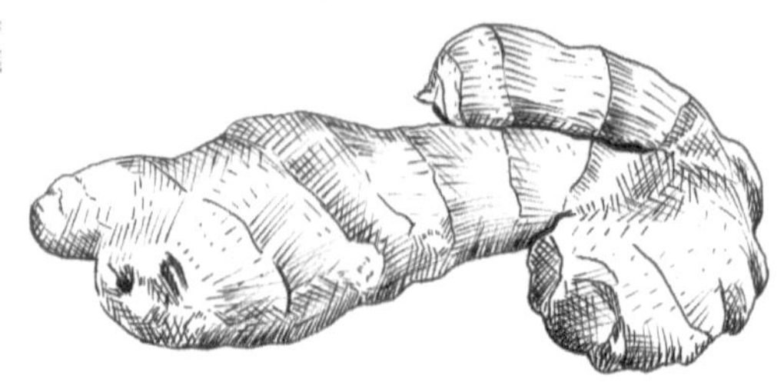

Healing Properties and Ancient and Modern Medicinal Use

Chemical analysis has shown that ginger or ginger oil contains hundreds of compounds and nowadays, scientists are examining the cause for the claims of centuries of therapeutic use and are finding that some claims may be true. Tests have shown that ginger tends to settle in the gastrointestinal tract which may give rise to its fame for reducing nausea like travel sickness or morning sickness in pregnant women. It is also effective in providing relief for the vomiting felt by chemotherapy patients, as effective as the conventional use of vitamin B6.

Some studies have shown that ginger can help to lower cholesterol in the blood, by assisting the liver to convert

cholesterol to bile acids, which can then be excreted easily. Other tests show that ginger can be useful to ease arthritis pain and inflammation, but studies have not confirmed this conclusively.

The US Food and Drug Administration recognizes ginger as a food additive and gingerol, a compound found in ginger root, is currently being tested for its anticancer properties. Tests have reported their ability to suppress the activity of some cancerous cells. Gingerol has been tested for its antioxidant properties.

Herbalists often recommend a piece of ginger in hot water first thing in the morning. In China and increasingly also in the west, hot tea is made with ginger and sweetened to chase away the common cold.

Where diarrhea is the problem, tests have shown that some ingredients in ginger can help to stop it and this is a useful, natural remedy in countries where prescription medication is not freely available for small children and adults alike. A piece of ginger can be put through a garlic crusher and added to warm water for even small children to help the stomach to settle.

Recipes, Tricks & Tips Using Ginger

Ginger is a versatile spice used for sweet or savory dishes.

Make candied ginger a few weeks before Christmas and use these as spicy decorations on cookies on the big day!

Instruction:

Use two pieces of 3-4 inches of fresh ginger root, peel it by cutting the brown edges off, and then slice the root into smaller shapes. Make the slices thin at a uniform width of ¼ of an inch.

Add these to a saucepan with 3 Tbsp of sugar and enough water to cover the ginger slices completely. Add a pinch of salt to this mixture, and then bring it to a boil. Allow to simmer at low heat for 20-30 minutes.

Now let's candy the pieces! So, let's add extra sugar, which also works as a preserving agent. I recommend adding 2 tsp to mix through the ginger pieces and the remaining water until the sugar dissolves.

Allow this to slow cook for 20-30 minutes but don't let the sugar burn, so stir and check frequently. Most of the liquid will be absorbed but drain the excess into a container for use later. Store your candied ginger in an airtight jar with a lid. They make a fantastic addition to a fresh cookie. Traditionally, ground ginger was only used in recipes. However, yours can have a unique purpose, using candied ginger shapes as decorations. Now let's make those cookies.

Gingerbread Biscuits

Serves: 4
Prep time: 30 minutes
Cook time: 10-15 minutes

Ingredients

- 12 oz/350 g plain flour
- 1 tsp baking soda
- 1 tsp ground ginger *or* 1 inch of fresh ground ginger root
- 1 tsp ground cinnamon
- 4 ½ oz / 125 g butter
- 4 oz /113 g butter, softened
- 4 Tbsp golden syrup *or* honey
- 1 egg
- Extra flour for dusting the rolling area

Suggestions for decorations: candied ginger, icing, marzipan shapes, etc.

Method

1. Sift the flour and baking soda into a mixing bowl.
2. Crush the fresh ginger if using, and grind into a powder.
3. Add ginger and cinnamon to the bowl and mix well.
4. Chop the butter into smaller pieces and mix into the flour to make breadcrumbs.
5. Add the sugar and stir well.

6. Beat the egg lightly in a cup, stirring to a smooth consistency, and add it to the bowl.
7. Drip in 4 Tbsp of golden syrup for that familiar sweetness. You can use honey instead if you prefer a natural sweetener. The taste will be slightly different.
8. You should have a dough by now, so knead it gently with your fingertips and then place it in a container to cool in the refrigerator for 15-30 minutes.
9. Set oven to 356°F/180°C.
10. Take the dough from the refrigerator and throw some flour on a clean surface where you will roll the mixture to make your gingerbread figures.
11. Use a rolling pin to make flat dough about 1 inch/2.5 cm thick. Use cookie cutters or a sharp knife to cut the shapes you want. Supervise young children doing this! You can make the traditional gingerbread man or woman or make Christmas trees, circles, or animals.
12. Bake the shapes for 10-15 minutes and keep a close eye on them because they burn quickly. You want them to look golden brown, so check after 10 minutes.
13. Remove from oven and place them on a wire tray to cool.
14. When they are cooler, decorate them with candied ginger, marzipan shapes, or chocolate treats. Use an icing bag for lines and make simple dots for eyes, nose, and mouth.
15. Store any uneaten biscuits in an airtight tin with a lid, and enjoy them over the festive season with a cup of tea whenever you like.

Biblical Herbs and Spices

From pagan times, humanity has long associated seasons with the celebration of the spring, summer, autumn, and winter solstices and equinoxes, and many traditions are related to these seasonal community gatherings, such as harvest meals. In countries where the four-season cycle is pronounced, the winter months are partly associated with Christmas, and therefore indirectly with the bible where our knowledge of herbs and spices is historically documented. Looking at the rich traditions revealed in the Bible, herbs and spices are mentioned as anointing herbs, for ceremonial celebrations, and as medicine, in addition to adding flavor to food.

Anointing oils were often used to purify and remove harmful elements. "Fragrant" Cinnamon is mentioned in Exodus 30:22-29, where it was mixed with herbs such as liquid Myrrh in olive oil as "sacred anointing oil". This was then used "to purify the tent of meeting, the ark of the covenant law, the table and all its articles" which included the altar and all the utensils. (**29** You shall consecrate them so they will be most holy, and whatever touches them will be holy.)

The benediction incense in churches uses a powerful scent, that fills a closed space in ceremonies. This

practice can provide a sacred space cleansed of exterior influence.

Frankincense *(Boswellia serrata)* is the tree that provides this oil and was one of the gifts brought by the Three Wise Men (The Magi) mentioned in Exodus 30:34 and Matthew 2:11. The spice was given to the newborn Jesus with other gifts of Myrrh and gold, showing the value of these spices at that time.

In Matthew 23:23 and Luke 11:42, the scent of Mint is referred. Mustard seed was used in Matthew 13:31-31 and 17:20. Perhaps the reference to Mint and Mustard refers to the wide availability of these plants in the area. Something that starts as tiny as a Mustard seed became a message to show that, with time, it eventually grows to become a larger plant with edible leaves for humans, and also as a food source for birds. The same idea is evident in the old saying that from a little acorn grows a very powerful large oak tree over many years. Many great things start as small ideas and just need time and nurturing.

Thyme is discussed in Luke 2:7, possibly because this is an herb of dry, sandy locations where it thrives almost in neglect. Tradition has it that the branches of thyme were placed in the manger to feed the sheep who lived in the stable where Jesus was born.

Passover herbs are the herbs eaten by Jews during the celebration of Passover. They celebrate escaping from Egypt into the land of Israel. These herbs are called bitter herbs, typically using chicory, endive, parsley, and watercress, but may include some of the following: celery, clover, dandelion leaves, horseradish, or onion.

For more stories about biblical herbs and a more extensive list, please check the resources at the end of this book.

Indoor and Outdoor Winter Herbs

Herbs you can Grow in the Colder Winter Months

I recommend 10 herbs for your winter season; basil, chives, cilantro, horseradish, parsley, rosemary, sage, tarragon, thyme, and winter savory. They were chosen either because they are hardy and survive winter outdoors or because they can happily grow indoors. All of these herbs provide tasty additions to winter cooking and they have a long history of use in kitchens worldwide in addition to medicinal benefits in the long, cold winter period. Here are some tips to care for them.

Before you plan your winter herbs, you need to understand the difference between an annual and a perennial herb and hardy and non-frost hardy plants.

1. *Annual herbs* (Basil, Cilantro) usually grow for just one season, from seed to plant to flower to seed. I will explain below how to help these survive the winter.
2. *Biennial herbs* (Parsley, Chicory) complete their life cycle in 2 years, growing foliage in year 1 and going to flower and seed in year 2.
3. *Perennial herbs* are those like sage, rosemary, and thyme which grow for years if you give them some sun, undisturbed. These often grow into shrubs

and bushes on a balcony or in your garden. Mint is another perennial but it dies back completely in winter but pops up again the following spring.

Frost hardy means a plant will survive a cold winter outdoors. You may have heard of USDA zones for hardiness. These levels measure how cold the average winter temperature is in a certain area and the zone number shows if your chosen herb can survive the coldest winter temperature in that area. So Basil is unlikely to tolerate temperatures of less than 32F and blackened leaves are often the result, if you forget to bring that pot indoors!

To identify the zone hardiness of your area in the US please refer to this link: https://planthardiness.ars.usda.gov/. For Canada, check: http://planthardiness.gc.ca/?m=1

The translation of these hardiness zones to Europe can be found under this reference:

https://www.gardenia.net/guide/
european-hardiness-zones

Buying and Conserving Herbs

Herbs can be found fresh in most supermarkets and stores or you can buy seeds and grow your own for maximum freshness. Herb oils usually store well but they gradually lose their taste and potency so discard them if you notice any mold or the oils start smelling `funny´.

All herbs presented in this book will keep for at least a week in the refrigerator if you wash them, wrap them in a dampened paper towel, and then in cling film. This way you can always cut off from the herb and then wrap the bunch again in the cling film and return it to the refrigerator.

The herbs last even longer in the freezer. Cut the spices with scissors into the size you use for your dishes. You can put them in freezer bags or cans and freeze them. Certain herbs are suitable to be portioned in ice cube containers with water, oil, or frozen in butter. This is recommended, for example, for chives or parsley.

Herbs can also be preserved by drying. Nevertheless, they should be consumed in 6-12 months, better in 2-3 months. To prepare, hang the bundles upside down in a dry and dust-free room. The room temperature should be between 70 - 85 F (20 - 30 degrees Celsius). Also, the room should be well- ventilated. The faster the plants dry, the better.

Alternatively, the herbs can be dried in the oven. For this, place the leaves of each plant on a baking sheet and dry them in the oven for about two to three hours at a maximum of 120F (50 degrees Celsius). The oven door should be left slightly ajar to allow the moisture to escape.

Basil, Osimum basilicum

History, Legends & Modern Times

Sweet Basil grows natively in India, where it is widely used for cooking. Basil was traded by spice merchants and soon it became established in Egypt, Rome, and Greece as both an herb and a medicinal plant. The Ancient Romans associated basil with Venus, the goddess of love, and used complex rituals to grow and collect it to ensure the herb retained maximum potency.

Many central European countries also have traditions with basil as a love potion. If a woman offers a sprig of basil to the man she has chosen, and the man accepts it, the belief is that he will fall in love with her.

In Greece, people carry some basil to celebrate St Basil's Day on the first day of January. Christians in Greece believed that the herb sprung up after the crucifixion of Jesus Christ, as a symbol of resurrection. Hindu belief is that basil is to accompany the dead to their afterlife home and that it can also be used for purification.

Single Line Sketch after the famous drawing of 'The Birth of Venus' 1483-1485 by Sandro Botticelli

Healing Properties and Ancient and Modern Medicinal Use

Basil leaves are an excellent source of calcium, magnesium, iron, and vitamins A, C, and K. It is a popular herb in cooking and also in medicine.

1. Pregnancy. Basil consumption is safe during pregnancy and is often advised for the nursing mother after birth, as a natural method of boosting breast milk production.
2. *Blood circulation.* Consuming fresh basil leaves was believed to improve blood circulation in general. Basil is an aid in lowering high cholesterol, and the magnesium it contains is diagnosed for its ability to relax muscles and blood vessels.
3. *Skin complaints.* Basil oil was used on a variety of insect bites as a soothing skin treatment. Some reports say it was used for snake bites as well. As a treatment for warts, an application of basil oil over several weeks is reported to remove them.
4. *Diabetes.* Research in India and other parts of Asia using extracts of basil leaves to lower blood sugar showed excellent results in diabetic rats and tests continue to determine whether basil could be useful for diabetic human patients.

Winter Gardening & How to Grow Basil Inside

Allow basil plants to grow outside as long as the weather is kind, but at the first sight of frost, either dig them up or move the pots indoors.

1. *Sow new seeds in late summer.* Basil sown in early summer will try to flower in August, and then goes to seed, so it is a good idea to sow fresh basil seeds towards the end of the summer to ensure you have new leaves for cutting indoors all winter long.
2. *Basil needs rich soil* and full sun indoors or out. Place several seeds per pot and water them well. The seeds are notoriously slow to germinate so be patient! To help them along, place them in an airing cupboard (or somewhere warm) to germinate but make sure the soil does not dry out.
3. As soon as they start growing, place the pot on a sunny windowsill but protect it at night when you normally pull the curtains.
4. If flower heads develop indoors, pick them and add them to salads - they are delicious. If you do not pick the flower, it will go to seed and you will need to start planting again.

Recipes, Tricks & Tips Using Basil

Basil is best used fresh, but you can freeze fresh basil leaves in an ice-cube tray and defrost them when you need its flavor. It's not as good as fresh leaves but acceptable for making pesto or any Italian dish that requires basil.

Decorate any cooked fish, like anchovies, with fresh basil for cold snacks to nibble at festive parties. Secure it with an olive to add the final Mediterranean touch.

Basil and Pine Nut Pesto

Pesto has its roots in ancient Rome. Throughout the Middle Ages, its simple version with lots of garlic was popular because, unlike expensive spices, herbs were tasty and cheap to procure. Also, their health benefits were acknowledged.

Serves: 4 or can be stored as garnish
Prep time: 20 minutes
Suitable for vegetarians who eat cheese.

Ingredients

- 1 cup fresh basil leaves
- ½ cup pine nuts
- 2 cloves garlic
- ½ cup olive oil
- ½ cup Parmesan cheese (grated)

- A pinch of black pepper and salt
- Lemon juice – optional

Method

1. Add all the ingredients to a food processor until it forms a smooth paste.
2. Store in the fridge for 5-7 days or longer in the freezer.

Chives, *Allium schoenoprasum*

History, Legends & Modern Times

Chives are known to have grown in Europe from the Middle Ages, but there is evidence of their usage as long as 5,000 years ago. No herb garden is really complete without a few fresh chives to make sauces or chive butter with! The spiky chopped leaves of chives have added flavors to sauces and salads.

Commonly seen as a charm to ward away the evil eye and diseases, like the Bubonic plague, bunches of chives were hung outside dwellings as protection in Central Europe. Chives were even used in fortune telling!

For the Romans, chives were used to soothe sore throats, and their use of chive oil to soothe skin complaints such as sunburn is still common.

In 1887, Vincent Van Gogh brought chives to the attention of the art community with his painting "Flowerpot with Garlic Chives".

These green spiky leaves are used in many countries from China to France, where they are one of the French 4 *Fines Herbes*; the others include tarragon, chervil, and sage.

Healing Properties and Ancient and Modern Medicinal Use

Chives are gorgeous in any flower bed. When the spiky green leaves go to flower, they produce purple round balls of color, like all members of the Allium family.

1. The leaves have high iron, calcium, and magnesium as well as a high vitamin C content. In addition, chives contain choline and folate, which are related to improving memory functions.
2. They also contain mustard oil which has been used medicinally for centuries to stimulate the appetite in patients with long-term illnesses and to aid digestion.
3. Chives have antibacterial and antiseptic properties and may be used as a diuretic, but do not use them as food at every meal. Added to soups, used as seasoning, or chopped into salads is fine.
4. Research shows that chives (and other members of the Allium family like garlic and onions) contain antioxidants that may help the body's immune response and reduce inflammation.

Winter Gardening & How to Grow Chives Inside

Chives are perennial outdoors to USDA zone 3 so if you sow them successfully, they will reappear every spring and you can harvest them right through to the fall when they die back in cooler temperatures unless you live in a very temperate climate.

To grow them successfully indoors, you need to sow some seeds in late August. They can be difficult to germinate so place them in a warm place and make sure the pot does not dry out. By September your pot should look green, full of tiny spiky chives so you can have fresh chives all year long.

It is a good idea to have 2 or 3 pots, sown at two-week intervals so that when you have picked most of the leaves in one pot you can turn to the next.

1. *Soil.* Chives need humus-rich soil and any extra compost or fertilizer usually encourages good growth.
2. *Light.* They need full sunlight indoors, on a south-facing window or similar, even though light will generally be lower in winter.
3. *Watering.* You need to check the soil to see if they need water but once a week is usually good. If the soil gets very dry due to central heating or being too hot indoors. You can always pop the whole plant outside for a few hours on a sunny day.
4. When spring arrives, you can replant the whole pot outdoors in a spot close to the kitchen.

Recipes, Tricks & Tips Using Chives

Bees adore chive flowers, which are pretty purple dots of color in your herb garden. You can use chive flowers in vases to make pretty flower arrangements.

Chives are high in vitamin C, so using them as a garnish or in a salad is a great way to keep healthy.

Do not use the same cutting board for chives, onions, garlic, or other herbs, because the robust and oniony flavor will taint other dishes. Have one cutting board for the onion family and one for everything else.

Chive and Lemon Cod

Fresh cod can taste bland, so chives and lemon add flavor, while the fresh chive garnish adds a bright green color to the dish, contrasting with the lemon zest. I like to serve this dish with butternut squash because the sweet, rich taste contrasts beautifully with the chives and fish.

Serves: 2
Prep time: 10 minutes
Cook time: 35 minutes

If you have more people, increase the fish per person and top up the fish stock with water. Allow 125 g of boneless cod per person.

Ingredients

- 1 large onion
- 2 Tbsp olive oil
- 1 Tbsp white flour
- 250 g of boneless cod (for 2 people)
- 60 ml white wine
- 150 ml fish stock
- Salt to taste
- A handful of chopped chives
- 1 lemon, squeezed, and some zest as garnish
- Chopped chives to garnish

Method

1. Remove the skin of the onion, chop it into small pieces and then fry in a pan for 3-4 minutes on medium heat in oil until golden.
2. Add the salt, sieve the flour into the pan, and cook gently, stirring all the while, so the flour does not go lumpy. This will thicken the sauce.
3. Add the white wine and the stock, stir to mix the ingredients all together, and then reduce the heat slightly.
4. Add the fish so it cooks gently until it is cooked through. This will take at least 15-20 minutes. If cooking from frozen, this stage may take longer. The fish should separate slightly when you touch it with a fork.

5. Add the chopped chives but reduce the heat to simmer for 5-10 minutes more.
6. Add the lemon juice only when the fish is cooked to retain all the vitamins.
7. To serve, add a sprinkling of fresh chives to each dish and some lemon zest.
8. Serve with fresh bread and butter or boiled potatoes. A side dish of butternut squash provides a colorful meal.

Cilantro, Coriandrum sativum

History, Legends & Modern Times

In the US, cilantro is the leafy green foliage that grows from the coriander seed whereas, in Europe, both the leaves and the seeds are known as coriander. This herb is a native of the Mediterranean and the Middle East but nowadays for its popular flavor, it is used worldwide.

Cilantro seeds were used as offerings in ancient burial rites. In 1993, The grave of the Siberian "Ice Maiden" was excavated in Pazyrk close to the Chinese border. This fifth-century BCE grave contained a woman's body dressed in fine clothing, carefully embalmed, and accompanied by horses. An offering bowl beside her coffin contained coriander seeds, presumably to accompany her to the next life.

Nowadays, cilantro is used in Brazilian, Egyptian, Indian, Mexican, European, Middle Eastern, Chinese, and Thai cooking for its distinctive taste.

Healing Properties and Ancient and Modern Medicinal Use

Cilantro leaves give you a full dose of vitamins A, C, E, and K, and they contain calcium, iron, magnesium, and potassium. They also have anti-inflammatory properties and contain useful phytonutrients.

Cilantro is known for its ability to cleanse and detox and this is often the reason it is included in smoothies for those who have consumed a little too much alcohol.

With increasing worries about toxic metals in drinking water, cilantro is said to aid kidney and liver functions by removing harmful minerals like aluminum, lead, and mercury by combining with them, which then allows the body to excrete them. Cilantro is sometimes offered to patients with cancer to help with disposing of these harmful substances.

Patients with measles and also those with painful toothache were offered cilantro in the past and it is also known as a digestive stimulant, perhaps for its delicious taste!

Winter Gardening & How to grow Cilantro inside

This plant provides the green leaves we know as cilantro and also seeds (coriander).

1. *Light.* It needs bright, direct sunshine and warmth and if you water it well indoors in a pot, you can keep this one going for most of the winter.
2. *Cilantro does tend to try to go to seed.* When there is a heatwave in summer cilantro assumes that water is short and often tries to flower. You will notice greenish-white (and sometimes pinkish) flowers and these need to be picked to stop the plant from going to seed.
3. Sometimes flowering cilantro may indicate that the plant has used up all the nutrients in its pot so you could change the soil and maybe give it a bigger pot and the plant should pick up its leaf production. However, I advise you to keep sowing new seeds for new plants as these are

more vigorous and then you can cut leaves to
your heart's content.

4. *Companion plant* cilantro in pots with tomatoes,
    chives, salads, or marjoram.

Recipes, Tricks & Tips Using Cilantro

You can keep a bunch of cilantro fresh by putting the stalks into a jar of water on the windowsill, so they do not wilt.

Mexican spicy green sauce gains its color from this herb using pre-cooked tomatillos, and the cilantro is added later.

Cilantro Spicy Green Sauce.

This recipe is inspired by 2 different sauces: Mexican green sauce and Korean Kimchi sauce. However, I add horseradish and ginger to make a super-hot taste on the tongue. These are optional, so if you prefer milder sauces, leave these last two out.

Serves: 6
Prep time: 10 minutes
Cook time: 10 minutes

Ingredients

- 1 lb fresh tomatillos (or just regular tomatoes)
- 1 cup fresh cilantro leaves
- 1 cup chopped onion
- 1 Tbsp fresh lime juice
- 2 hot chili peppers (with seeds)
- A pinch of salt

Optional

- Garlic – use 2 cloves
- 2-inch piece of ginger root
- 2-inch piece of horseradish root
- 1 Tbsp white vinegar

Method

1. First, cook the tomatillos by grilling or baking them. Their skins will turn slightly brown or black, but this adds to the flavor.
2. Use 1 cup of fresh cilantro leaves and chop them finely.
3. You can bulk up the green color with spinach, kale, or cabbage leaves but make sure these are blanched in boiling water first.
4. Place all the ingredients in a food processor and whizz them with a tiny bit of water or white wine vinegar to make a smooth paste.
5. If using, peel the skin from the horseradish (or ginger) and add some chopped pieces, and whizz again.
6. Add it as a garnish on anything you like. It will store happily in a refrigerator for a week.
7. Serve with cold meats, cheese, or soup dishes with bread.

INDOOR AND OUTDOOR WINTER HERBS

Horseradish, Amoracia ruticana

History, Legends & Modern Times

The spicy zing of horseradish in sauce or cooking is common nowadays in Asia, Europe, and the US. This plant is part of the *Brassicacae* family. The taste of horseradish root is described as spicy, with a touch of mustard but strangely also slightly sweet so the tongue feels heat and the eyes may water!

The use of horseradish as a medicine is mentioned by Dioscorides (40-90 AD), the Ancient Greek botanist who was employed by the Roman army, in his famous herbal *"De Materia Medica"* which is still widely consulted today. This collection of books about the use of herbs as medicine is called a pharmacopeia.

European herbalists used horseradish internally but also as a poultice for external use on sports injuries, and muscles and nerves affected by arthritis. This was also a tradition of the Ancient Greeks who used it externally for congestion by placing the poultice of grated herb on the chest until the patient felt a warming or a burning feeling on the chest or lungs. The tincture is often used for sore throats in many European and Asian countries.

In the Middle Ages, the herb accompanied oysters and beef. Nowadays, horseradish is an ingredient used inwedding dishes in Bavaria, Germany. In Albania horseradish is added to pickled pears as a preservative. In the Czech Republic and Slovakia, horseradish is added to cooking so that the taste is diffused throughout the dish and is therefore less spicy.

Native American usage was to avoid scurvy, as a digestive stimulant, and to treat influenza, congestion, and the common cold. All of these uses concur with European usage at the same time.

Healing Properties and Ancient and Modern Medicinal Use

Horseradish is a hardy perennial plant in zones 2-9 with large, glossy, pointed, green leaves aboveground, which appear in spring if it is grown outdoors.

Leaves are eaten in Asia, but it is the root that is approved for medical use by the British Pharmacopeia and the German Commission E, which is the scientific advisory board of the Federal Institute for Drugs and Medical Devices formed in 1978.

In tests, the root is shown to be antiseptic, and this may be why it is used externally for congestion and to ease muscle or arthritis pain. It has stimulant and diuretic effects, which may explain why it was used to help with urinary

and kidney conditions. It contains glucosinolates, which have been shown to improve liver function and promote healthy cell growth.

It is recommended for external use for aches and pains or for treating muscle aches by applying a poultice of fresh root collected in linen or cloth and applied directly to the area until the person feels a warm, burning sensation on the skin. The essential oil, which contains a higher concentration of active ingredients, is useful in massage for arthritic pain for treating congestion and sore throats, in many European countries.

Winter Gardening & How to Grow Horseradish Inside

Horseradish grows in sunny places in southwestern Europe, and it enjoys rich soil but it may become invasive. The leaves die back in winter but the roots continue growing underground so most gardeners prefer to grow them in a deep pot or to dig up the roots every fall to prevent the invasion. You can continue to dig up fresh roots as long as the ground is not frozen and also freeze some for use.

Taking a plant indoors allows it to believe that summer has not ended, so it will continue to grow fresh. Horseradish adores full sun so give it a warm, sunny location like a conservatory or a south-facing window and a deep pot, at least 1 foot (30 cm) with rich soil to keep it content.

Harvest the root by gently digging at the base of the leaves and then cut a small piece for immediate use. The plant should not be affected and will continue to grow.

Recipes, Tricks & Tips Using Horseradish

An interesting characteristic of the root is that no compounds are released until it is cut or ground, at which point your eyes will stream, as isothiocyanates are released during the grating and crushing of the root. Adding vinegar (or milk) will stop this chemical reaction and the flavor at that level will be maintained. This mixture is also traditionally used to remove sunspots or freckles as a natural bleach.

Tonic. In Germany, taking 20g of fresh root orally daily is suggested for adults to maintain good health. The British Pharmacopoeia recommended a mulled wine for help in "languid digestion". The recipe includes grated root, orange peel, and nutmeg, and "spirit of wine" was recommended for rheumatism.

One difference some people may not be aware of is the one between horseradish and parsnip. While they both have whitish roots, they taste completely different. Parsnip is a biennial plant belonging to a family of mostly aromatic flowering plants (Apiaceae, formally Umbelliferae), while 'horseradish' belongs, as pointed out by the name, to the 'radish family', being an edible root (*Raphanus sativus*). The in-depth comparison of the nutritional values is given in the footers website reference.

Fresh horseradish is a fantastic ingredient because you can just dig up a small amount of the root when needed. It's an ingredient in Wasabi sauce, the spicy Japanese condiment served with sushi.

Parsnip (or Potato) and Horseradish Soup

Serves: 2
Prep time: 10 minutes
Cook time: 30 minutes

Ingredients

- 2 parsnip roots (or use any root vegetable you like, e.g., potatoes)
- 2 cups (450 ml) water to cover the roots
- 1 large onion, peeled
- 2 cloves of garlic, peeled
- Salt to taste
- 1 cup (250 ml) white wine
- 1 cup (250 ml) chicken stock (or vegetable)
- 2-inch piece of fresh horseradish root, peeled and chopped

Method

1. Wash and chop the parsnips, horseradish, onion, and garlic and add these to a saucepan filled with enough water to cover the roots. Add a pinch of salt.
2. Cook these gently for 15 minutes until they start to go soft. Add the wine and the stock, and then use a food processor to achieve a smooth consistency to the soup.

3. The flavor of the horseradish will be evident even though it is cooked.
4. To serve, add the soup to 4 bowls and top with plain yogurt and warm toast. Great after a long cold winter walk.

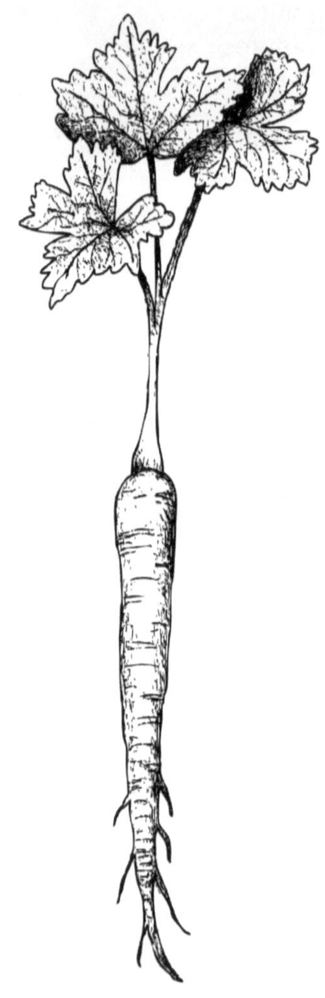

Parsnip

  INDOOR AND OUTDOOR WINTER HERBS

Parsley, Petroselinum crispum

History, Legends & Modern Times

The origin of the word parsley comes from the original Greek πετροσέλινον (*petroselinon*), which was translated into Latin as *petroselinium*. The Old English and German words for the herb were the same; *petersilie* while the French word was *peresil* and the Spanish *perejil*. Somehow parsley is now the accepted word for this wonderful herb and is widely used in all five continents.

This herb can be confusing as there are several varieties; moss curled leaf parsley and flat leaf parsley both share the same name. In Europe, there is also Hamburg (or root) parsley, which allows for leaf cuts in the summer but also supplies a root vegetable in the winter. Italian parsley has a stronger taste than the ones available in the US.

Parsley and Hamburg Parsley

Parsley is eaten in Brazil, where chopped parsley with green onions is known as *cheiro-verde* (literally green aroma). Parsley is adored in Italy, in Europe as part of the sprig of herbs for "Bouquet Garni" used to flavor slow-cooked casseroles and soups. In Asia parsley is used as a garnish and chopped into dishes. In England, its taste makes parsley sauce, and it is one of the 4 herbs used in the French *Fines Herbes* while *Salsa Verde* in Italy contains parsley with garlic, capers, and anchovies to make this unique taste. It also appears as a green garnish on many dishes.

Healing Properties and Ancient and Modern Medicinal Use

Parsley foliage can vary from the curly parsley we often use as garnish, to the broader leaves of flat-leaved parsley or the even larger Root parsley that grows in Europe. The fresh leaves of all types of parsley are full of nutrients; they contain antioxidants and flavonoids as well as vitamins A, C, and K and they are a good source of alpha *and* beta carotene. Parsley seeds are used in cooking in some parts of the world and they add a strong flavor to any cooked dish.

During pregnancy, women need to restrict the amount of parsley they eat because it can affect uterus muscles that protect the baby if large amounts are eaten.

Winter Gardening & How to Grow Herbs Inside

Although seed packets tell you that Parsley is biennial, (meaning it takes two years to complete its life cycle), I recommend growing it as an annual. It may survive outdoors in warmer climates but my advice for winter growing is always to sow seed in spring and then sow *again* in August and September, which gives you parsley a month apart to use in the winter kitchen.

1. *Germination.* Parsley can grow beautifully indoors as long as you can get it to germinate. It enjoys rich compost but do not water the pot too much as this herb will not tolerate cold, wet soil. Keep your seeds cozy in the airing cupboard, covered with a plastic bag. and check them each day. As soon as green shoots appear, move the pot onto a windowsill.

2. *Light.* Parsley enjoys the sun but prefers some shade in the hottest part of the day. However, winter temperatures are rarely as hot as summer so indoors this is unlikely to be a problem.

3. *Watering.* Give parsley a windowsill with some light and water well if the plant seems to wilt during the day. Once established, you can pick leaves as you please.

4. *If spring arrives and your parsley still looks good,* you can plant it back out in the garden or on your balcony. Hopefully, it will self-seed and you will have a constant supply!

Recipes, Tricks & Tips Using Parsley

Parsley is a universal garnish, adding its green, unique shape and taste to dishes worldwide.

The French added parsley to spice mixtures known as "Bouquet Garni," which typically consists of tarragon, parsley, chives, and chervil. "Fines herbs" come from a region in southeast France called "Provence." The spice mixture often has the same herbs as Bouquet Garni, but rosemary, thyme, and oregano also may be mixed in.

Parsley sauce, also known as white sauce, combines a roux base with the leaves to flavor fish dishes in Mediterranean countries.

Parsley butter uses fresh leaves in a butter mixture to melt on steaks or meat dishes.

Parsley adds a unique taste to homemade paté, and a vegetarian version can be made using cooked broad beans as a meat substitute. Beans provide protein and a festive green color, while the fresh parsley leaves add a distinctive flavor to this paté.

Parsley and Broad Bean Patê

Serves: 4
Prep time: 30 minutes
Cook time: 15 minutes

Ingredients

- 1 cup fresh broad beans
- 3 sprigs parsley, chopped
- 1 clove garlic
- 1 Tbsp tahini (a paste made from sesame seeds, used in Mediterranean and Middle Eastern cuisine)
- Salt and pepper to taste
- 1 sprig of parsley per person to garnish

Method

1. Add the beans and a clove of garlic to a saucepan with enough water to cover the beans.
2. Cook until the beans are soft (15-20 minutes), then drain and remove the skins.
3. Chop the parsley while the beans are cooking and drop chopped parsley into the water after 10 minutes.
4. Either use a fork to mash the beans and garlic into a smooth consistency or place in a food processor for 2 minutes.
5. Add the tahini and the salt and pepper to taste.

6. Serve with crackers or bread, cheese, and a fresh salad. Garnish with a sprig of parsley.
7. Store in a covered bowl, and it will keep in the fridge for 4-5 days, but I doubt it will last that long!

Rosemary, Salvia Rosmarinus

History, Legends & Modern Times

Rosemary in Latin means "the dew of the sea" possibly referring to the colors of its flowers or its location on Mediterranean shorelines. It has a delicious scent, and cosmetics frequently add it to bring depth to the scent.

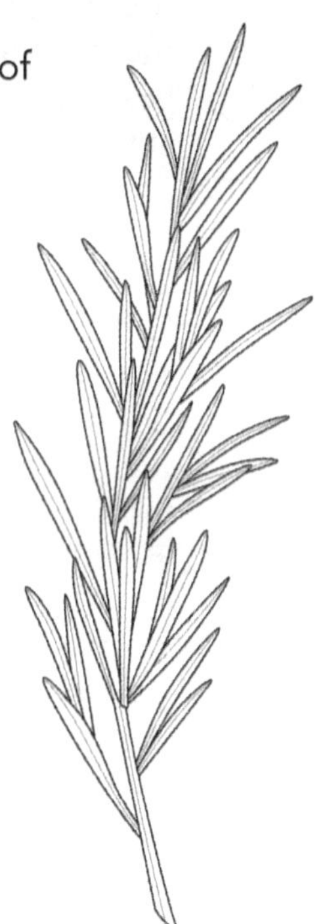

Traditionally it was used to ease sore muscles and soothe inflammation by Native American people and this medicinal use of the herb is common.

Its delightful scent in saunas and steam rooms makes this essential oil very popular worldwide.

Healing Properties and Ancient and Modern Medicinal Use

Rosemary comes from the same family as sage and when you look at both shrubs, you can see woody stems and smell them a mile away. Both herbs have flowers that bees adore.

This shrub can grow as tall as 2-3 feet (60-90 cm) and spread horizontally almost to fit available space.

Use Rosemary for:

1. *Gout* is a common form of inflammatory arthritis, that is very painful. It usually affects one joint at a time (often the big toe joint). There is a long history of using rosemary for gout and there are written records of its use in several herbal medicine manuscripts from the ninth century onwards and later herbalists also report using it to help gout sufferers.

2. *Easing muscle pain*. Rosemary is widely used to help inflammation and it has antibacterial, antifungal, antioxidative, and antiviral properties.

3. *Food preservation*. Rosemary oil helped to preserve food in the days before refrigeration because it contains rosemary oleoresin, which was used in preserving meat. It can be used in the same way today.

4. *In the UK,* rosemary was used to bring down high temperatures in fevers and the essential oil was applied directly for toothache.

5. Some sixteenth-century records exist of the use of rosemary as an herb to smoke! It was made by combining leaves with other herbs and then crushing them into a type of tobacco. Nowadays, we would not treat lung conditions in this way and this is not advisable.

6. *Eyewashes and conjunctivitis treatment.* In Asia, an infusion of the leaves is used to clear the eye in mild allergic reactions or as a natural treatment for conjunctivitis. This is an inflammation or infection of the transparent membrane (conjunctiva) that lines your eyelid and covers the white part of your eyeball.

7. *Scent.* In saunas, rosemary is commonly used for its distinctive scent in many countries. The strong scent is used in toothpaste and cosmetics and soaps.

8. *Aromatherapy* often uses rosemary for ear infections and better liver function.

Winter Gardening & How to
Grow Rosemary Inside

Rosemary is quite a hardy herb, and my advice is to leave it in the ground outdoors during the winter, if possible. If taking it indoors, give it a deep pot and make sure the soil has good drainage and contains some sand, like those Mediterranean coastlines. *This shrub will need annual pruning* in a garden situation to keep it in check, but in a pot indoors, rosemary can be limited to the nutrients contained in the soil.

When you prune you can either dry the cut branches and leaves for use in the kitchen or use them to make new plants.

After two years the flowers will arrive in late spring so expect blue beauties and a swarm of bees, ladybugs, and pollinators with them!

For multiplying when you prune your bush, add some hormone rooting powder to the end of the cut stems and then place several in soil in a pot. If you prefer a natural rooting agent, cut an Aloe Vera leaf and use the gel from the interior on the end of the pruned sticks. At least one should take! Take these pots indoors if you like and you can pick fresh herbs whenever you like.

Outdoors in winter, your Rosemary plant will sometimes look frostbitten after snow or a severe frost. The tips of the branches can even turn a darker brown color. Don't panic. Even if this happens, the roots will remain safe underground and in spring, the tips will start growing again.

Recipes, Tricks & Tips Using Rosemary

Rosemary croquettes can be made with any leftover potato and meat – just combine the ingredients with a few leaves and an egg. Coat them with the egg and fry gently at high heat in a fryer for a crunchy snack or as party food.

Rosemary Veggie Nut Loaf
(Made with Leftovers)

Use leftover bread stuffing from Christmas dinner to make a nut loaf, provided that no meat or dairy products are included. Use olive oil instead of butter for vegans, and you can also try Quorn as the protein content. This fermented fungus resembles cheese in vegan and vegetarian cooking. Adding fresh rosemary to the mix brings out its unique flavor for a slow-cooked roast dinner for vegans and vegetarians, but I guarantee you that everybody will want to try this one!

Serves: 4
Prep time: 40 minutes
Cook time: 60 minutes

Ingredients Vegetarian

- 1 onion
- 3 cloves of garlic
- 1.05 oz (30 g) butter
- 1 Tbsp olive oil
- 7 oz (200 g) breadcrumb stuffing *or*

- 4 slices of bread, crumbed *or*
- 5 oz (150 g) of mushrooms
- 7 oz (200 g) nuts of your choice (walnuts, cashews, almonds)
- 2 eggs, one to coat the outside and the other mixed in
- 2 fresh, long sprigs of rosemary
- Salt and pepper to taste

Method.

1. Preheat oven to 360°F/ 180°C.
2. Peel the onions and garlic and then chop them into thin slices.
3. Add olive oil to the saucepan and cook garlic and onions for about 5 minutes or until they are a honey-brown color.
4. Chop the mushrooms into even slices and cook for 10 minutes.
5. Next, add the breadcrumbs and nuts to make the loaf.
6. If you prefer your nuts smooth, grind them in the food processor. I like them slightly crunchy, so I chop bigger walnuts. However, I leave whole cashews, so this depends on the nuts you choose.
7. Add salt and pepper and use one of the eggs to stir into the mixture to bind it together. The other egg will be used to coat the outside of the loaf.
8. Finally, chop the rosemary into smaller pieces and stir this into the dough.
9. Place the mixture in a baking loaf tray or on parchment paper on a baking tray and form the mixture into the shape you like.
10. Place it in the oven and cook for 60 minutes.

11. Serve slices of the loaf with fresh salad and a cheeseboard. Leftover meats can be added for non-vegetarians.

Ingredients Vegan

- 1 onion
- 3 cloves of garlic
- 2 Tbsp olive oil
- 4 slices of vegan bread, crumbed *or*
- 7 oz (200 g) of cooked lentils
- 2 Tbsp almond milk
- 5 oz (150g) mushrooms
- 7 oz (200 g) Quorn (or tofu)
- 7 oz (200 g) nuts of your choice (walnuts, cashews, almonds)

Method

1. Heat the oven to 360°F (180°C).
2. Line the base and sides of a 1.5-liter loaf pan with parchment paper.
3. Use crushed nuts and Quorn to make the base; any nuts you prefer.
4. The nuts provide a pleasant back taste on which the rosemary will infuse.
5. To make a vegan nut roast, use an extra Tbsp of oil instead of butter, no cheese, and 3 Tbsp of egg substitute. Bake your nut roast for 1 hour. The loaf will still be soft in the middle after cooking.

Sage, Salvia officinalis

History, Legends & Modern Times

For Native Americans, four herbs were given as gifts to humans from the Creator. These are known as the Four Sacred Medicines. The first was tobacco and sage was the second gift followed by cedar and sweetgrass completed the four. Sage is still frequently used in ceremonies to purify space and in Sweat Lodges and "smudging" practices; this involves lighting sage as incense or sometimes added to grass bundles, to scent the air, offer thanks, help to purify the atmosphere, and finally, for protection against unwanted or evil influences.

Sage is also a common herb in American herbal gardens and is valued worldwide for its gorgeous scent but also for its medicinal qualities.

Healing Properties and Ancient and Modern Medicinal Use

Sage plants grow into sturdy shrubs in their native Mediterranean but and it has been introduced all over the world. In traditional medicine, it has been used as an anti-inflammatory, and its scent is used in cosmetics as well as cooking.

1. *You can eat a sage leaf fresh* from the plant to benefit from its antiseptic properties, but it is more commonly added to flavor soups, stuffing, and hot casserole dishes.
2. *For sore throats and gums,* you can add some sage leaves to a cup of boiling water and allow it to cool, and then gargle with it twice a day. Sage provides some antiseptic qualities.
3. *Coughs, colds, and bronchitis.* Sage oil and sage tea are commonly used to treat asthma and the common cold, coughs, and bronchitis
4. *Muscle relaxant.* Sage essential oil has antiseptic and antispasmodic properties. Oil can be used to massage muscles to help them relax after sport or a long day at work!
5. The antioxidant components of sage include rosmarinic and chlorogenic acid (yes, they also are constituents of sage), and rutin, which are believed to aid memory function, and perhaps lower the risk of cancer.
6. Infusions of sage leaves are often recommended for menopause symptoms and as a tonic for depression.
7. Current research in Asia (particularly in China and India) suggests that the use of the herb may also include natural remedies for healthy heart

function, diabetes, and relief from a range of long-term conditions from depression to lupus.

Winter Gardening & How to Grow Sage Inside

Sage usually does not need to be moved inside in winter as it is a very hardy shrub in USDA zone 5. This herb grows into a middle-sized shrub but it can expand over time so keep an eye on it because it may need pruning every year. You can save these pruned branches and dry the leaves for winter use and the twigs smell wonderful burned on a wood-burning stove or chimenea.

1. *You can move a pot indoors* if you like but you need to allow it enough space to thrive in a pot so choose the biggest pot to suit the space available.
2. *Outdoor sage plants* tend to dominate any soil they are in by emitting substances to deter the growth of certain plants via their roots. If you are short of space, then compatible plants to accompany sage are strawberries or borage. These three provide bees with wonderful flowers to pollinate.
3. Choose a sunny spot indoors or outside, and do not water sage too much.
4. *Soil.* It prefers soil with a bit of sand and it must be well-drained because sage roots do not enjoy being wet.

Recipes, Tricks & Tips Using Sage

Sage accompanies duck and goose really well, and its intense flavor is excellent with veal and pork too.

When you prune your sage bush, dry out some branches and cut them into sizes to fit a wood-burning stove or an outdoor fire. The scent is wonderful.

An old wives tale says a sage leaf every day is good for women's health. I follow this advice as I pass by the bush, and it certainly feels good for me.

Roast Turkey with Orange and Sage

Serves: 6
Prep time: 20 minutes
Cook time: Depends on the weight of your bird

Ingredients

- ½ cup unsalted butter at room temperature
- 12- to 14-pound turkey, giblets removed
- Zest of 1 orange
- 2 cloves garlic, minced
- 2 Tbsp chopped fresh sage
- 1 Tbsp kosher salt, plus more to taste
- ½ bottle dry white wine (375 ml)
- 12 fresh sage leaves
- 1 tsp freshly ground black pepper, plus more to taste
- 2 cups orange juice

Method

1. Heat oven to 400°F (200°C).
2. Prepare the turkey:
3. Spot the turkey on a rack in a roasting pan after patting it dry with paper towels.
4. The turkey's legs should be tied together using butcher's twine, and its wings should be folded under the bird.
5. Place a meat thermometer into the thickest section of the animal. Make sure it does not touch the bone.
6. Mash the butter with the sage, garlic, salt, and pepper to make a paste in a small basin or on a clean chopping board.
7. To gently separate the skin from the breast meat, lift the turkey's skin at the neck. Cover the breast meat with roughly half of the butter mixture rubbed under the skin.
8. Add some extra salt and pepper after applying the remaining butter to the turkey's skin.
9. After adding the sage leaves to the wine and orange juice in the roasting pan, carefully place the pan in the oven.
10. Roast for around two to three hours; baste with drippings every thirty minutes. Start monitoring the turkey 1 hour and 45 minutes into the cooking process. If the skin is getting very brown, tent it with foil.
11. Cook until the instant-read thermometer reads 330°F (165°C).
12. Before carving, move the meat to a cutting board or dish and give it at least 30 minutes to rest.

Tarragon, Artemisia dracunculus

History, Legends & Modern Times

There are two types of tarragon, French tarragon, and Russian tarragon. Sadly, the Russian cousin does not offer the same taste as the French. (French) Tarragon is an essential herb in France, as one of the 4 herbs used in *Fines Herbes*, a mixture containing chives, chervil, parsley, and tarragon.

Although the French lay claim to tarragon, it is not native to France. Originally, the herb grew in Mongolia and Siberia and was it brought by the Crusaders to Europe to trade. In Mongolia, it was used to flavor food but also as an herb that would help you to sleep soundly. They also used it as natural toothpaste, and anybody familiar with its taste will agree that it certainly brings an anise-flavored zing to the mouth.

The first part of the Latin name refers to Artemis, the goddess of the moon for the Ancient Greeks. Legend has it that Chiron gave the herb to Artemis.

France claims a long history of cooking with this herb and the French name *Herbe au Dragon* refers to the second part of the Latin name, *dranuculus,* meaning little or small dragon. Italy calls the herb *dragoncello*, so here it is known as the dragon herb too. The dragon referred to may be the root of the tarragon plant, which strangely curves into the shape of a dragon with a little imagination.

Siena, in Italy, is famous for the use of tarragon in local recipes, and dishes that are cooked in a Sienese style will tell you that they contain tarragon.

Healing Properties and Ancient
and Modern Medicinal Use

Tarragon is recommended in the history books for nausea, flatulence, and to flavor egg custards which were soft on the tongue and easy to eat. This food was offered to long-term invalids reluctant to eat. Poor digestion was said to be eased with a sprinkling of tarragon contained in the prepared dish.

It has been used as medicine for a range of medical conditions from arthritis to gout. Saint Catherine is reported as bringing tarragon as a gift on a visit to Pope Clement VI in the fourteenth century, but nobody is sure if it was for seasoning or medicinal use.

Its essential oil with aniseed flavor was used to rub directly on toothaches. This is similar to the use of clove oil for toothaches. Both leave a tingling numbing sensation and they may have been a good emergency treatment when no dentist was available.

Historically, tarragon was also used to soothe insect bites, snake bites, stings, and dog bites for the same reason. If you make your own oil, be aware that tarragon oil needs to be very fresh and the scent of the herb is quickly lost in essential oil.

Winter Gardening & How to Grow Tarragon Inside

Tarragon is hardy in USDA zone 3 but be very wary of this herb getting frostbite. Experienced gardeners often say you can leave it outdoors to overwinter. This is because the plant tends to die back but new spikes will emerge the following spring so don't worry too much! This is the herb's natural method of protection from the colder winter months. I advise a layer of mulch over the herb as it starts to die back. This can be straw, grass, or compost but nothing too rich because this herb likes poor soil in my experience.

If you fancy a taste of tarragon indoors, then cut a section of the plant with a root or prune a few twigs from your plant in late summer and place these in a pot filled with soil to root, which can then be taken indoors.

1. *Light.* Offer your tarragon plant the best sunny spot and the herb will reward you with many new leaves to pick.
2. *Soil.* It is quite a fussy plant to transplant. Make sure the soil is not too rich, and especially that you do not overwater.
3. *Watering.* Always check the soil to see how dry it is first. This herb really hates wet roots, so drain away any excess in a tray or saucer indoors and then pour this away or use it on another plant.

If you follow these instructions, you can pick leaves all winter.

Recipes, Tricks & Tips Using Tarragon

Fresh leaves are definitely the best! Try to have an indoor plant to use.

Tarragon vinegar is adored in France, and the unique flavor is used on salads to add a certain savory something.

Tarragon, as a sweet herb, is widely used in French cooking too, where it is used to flavor custards. A famous one is *Crème anglaise*, which roughly translates to English egg custard or is sometimes known as a drinking custard in the U.S.

Tarragon Brussels Sprouts

I love the flavors of these two together! The subtle sweetness of the herb adds an interesting back-taste to the sprouts, particularly if there are leftover cooked sprouts from the day before. Served on warm toast, these can be eaten with cheese and olives for a light lunch.

Serves: 2
Prep time: 10 minutes
Cook time: 10-15 minutes

Ingredients

- Leftover brussels sprouts
- 1 onion
- 1 clove of garlic
- 1 Tbsp olive oil
- Black pepper
- 1 tsp fresh tarragon leaves
- Toasted bread to serve

Method

1. Peel and chop the onion and garlic and fry them in olive oil in a saucepan at medium heat (250-304°F/121-162°C).
2. Chop the leftover cooked brussels sprouts in half. You'll need 5 minutes longer cook time if you use fresh sprouts.
3. Use black pepper to taste, and you can add some to the served dish, too.
4. Add the tarragon leaves after the black pepper and then cook steadily for 5 minutes on low heat (120-150°F/48-65°C) to conserve the delicate fragrance.
5. Serve with eggs for lunch or as a side dish with cheese and cold cooked lunch meat. Delicious with warm toast.

Thyme, Thymus vulgaris

History, Legends & Modern Times

Thyme and Rosemary are often used in the kitchen at the same time, and these two were twinned for use in making soups, often tied together in a *"Bouquet Garni"* and removed just before serving.

Thyme is also mentioned in the well-known English folk song "Are you going to Scarborough fair?", where the singer wonders if the listener is going to buy parsley, sage, rosemary, and thyme.

A custom in England in the Middle Ages was to give a soldier a sprig of thyme before going to war, making use of the scent in a pocket to remind them of sweet herbs growing in gardens back home. This was also customary in Rome, where it was said to inspire courage in the soldier.

In Rome, thyme was also seen as a defense against poison. In the time of the Roman Emperor Julius Caesar, poisoning was common, so thyme was part of the meal for the prudent, just in case.

In hospitals, thyme or thyme oil was sometimes used on wounds before applying a plaster. Modern research confirms that thyme has antiseptic qualities.

The use of thyme in embalming dates back to the Egyptians, who used its scent and its ability to mummify and preserve a body. In Egypt, thyme was also recommended for relieving pain as one of its effects is to sedate you with the scent. Try picking a sprig of fresh herb and rubbing it gently to release the oil and you can see what I mean.

Healing Properties and Ancient and Modern Medicinal Use

Thyme aromatic essential oil is antiseptic and can be used on a wound in an emergency. It was used topically in hospitals in Europe for centuries in this way.

The oil contains thymol and tests show that it contains antibacterial, antifungal, antiviral, antispasmodic, and sedative qualities. The Egyptians were not wrong to use it as a sedative and this herb is packed with good medicinal properties as well as good taste.

Nowadays thymol is added to cough mixtures as an expectorant and to disinfectants to purify and clean surfaces. Its historic use in preserving food is backed up by modern science, as it has been shown to prolong the life of foods it is added to.

As a natural sedative, taken as an infusion it will help insomnia sufferers and even calm nightmares for younger children.

Winter Gardening & How to Grow Thyme Inside

Thyme is a native of the Mediterranean and there are about 300 different types but they all share that thyme taste. You can leave it outdoors in winter for most locations in the US and Europe, apart from the coldest parts of Scandinavia. It is hardy to zone 4 so will survive temperatures as low as -30F (-34 degrees Celsius).

I recommend leaving it outdoors if you can, so you can pick fresh leaves whenever you like. It is usually bought as a small herb in a pot but when planted in soil, it expands rapidly and can become quite straggly and leggy in a couple of years.

You can divide the plant by digging it up in the autumn and splitting the plant (including roots) in two, then re-pot one for indoors and re-plant the other in its spot outdoors. This way, you can pick indoors and if the winter is very harsh, you can still have thyme the following summer.

1. Your thyme can be picked in winter but it will not be growing in this period so you can add mulch (like straw or hay) around any plant that will be exposed to low temperatures.
2. *Pick it when you need it.* The aromatic oil in thyme leaves is more likely to be full of vitamins when it is freshly picked by you, on a cold winter's day to add to soups, stews, stuffing, or sprinkled on egg dishes.
3. *Soil* does not need to be rich; it prefers sandy, well-drained soil almost thriving on neglect!

4. *Take cuttings*. Be warned that an old thyme plant may need you to take cuttings as the whole plant can just die back after 4-5 years from old age. If you take cuttings in the fall, you can take these pots indoors if you like. This means you can replace old plants with these cuttings.

Recipes, Tricks & Tips Using Thyme

Rub thyme onto poultry – also good on fish -- before cooking. However, due to its distinctive taste, use sparingly.

Thyme and Eggplants/Aubergine Cheese Bake

Serves: 4
Prep time: 10 minutes
Cook time: 20 minutes

Ingredients

- 2 eggplants (aubergines U.K.), chopped into round slices
- 3 cloves of Garlic
- 2 Tbsp Olive oil
- Several sprigs of thyme to cook on top
- Salt and black pepper to taste

Method

1. Heat the oven to 360°F (180°C)
2. Eggplants (aubergines) tend to caramelize if you cook them in the oven, so this recipe pre-bakes them, and the thyme is cooked on top for its subtle flavors.
3. Chop the eggplant into round slices and sprinkle them with olive oil. You will have a lot, so make

sure you have a large baking tray or two ready. Sprinkle half of the thyme leaves on top of the oil to allow them to make their mark on the dish.

4. Bake for 20 minutes until the eggplant/aubergine feels soft. Remove them from the oven and allow them to cool.

5. Take half of the cooked eggplant/aubergine slices and mash them with a fork into a creamy mixture.

6. Peel and cut the garlic into thin pieces and fry it in the olive oil on low heat for 2 minutes. As soon as it looks honey-colored, add the mashed vegetables to simmer gently for 2 minutes more.

7. Season with salt and black pepper and add some fresh thyme. Check with your guests if they enjoy fresh thyme, though. Some people enjoy the flavor but not chewing the leaves.

8. Remember to cook both sides of the eggplant/aubergine! Turn them over in the pan during cooking and season again.

9. To serve, eat with rice or between two slices of bread as a packed lunch for work or school.

INDOOR AND OUTDOOR WINTER HERBS

Winter Savory, *Satureja hortensis and - montana*

History, Legends & Modern Times

Perennial Winter Savory and annual Summer Savory offer the herb grower a challenge. The winter herb is extremely spicy compared to its summer equivalent. Both the leaves and the flowers are edible and have been used to preserve food for centuries in Europe and the Mediterranean. Its antibacterial properties have been proven by modern testing.

The Latin name of this herb *Satureja* was given by Pliny (23-79AD). He named the plant after the mythical satyrs, we often call Chiron a half man, half wild animal. Chiron was a healer and he originally tended plants to make medicine but the satyrs also lived close to Dionysus, who is famed for his love of wine and the pleasure of food, sex, and the art of dance. Sensual pleasure is the essence of this herb which was frequently taken as an aphrodisiac.

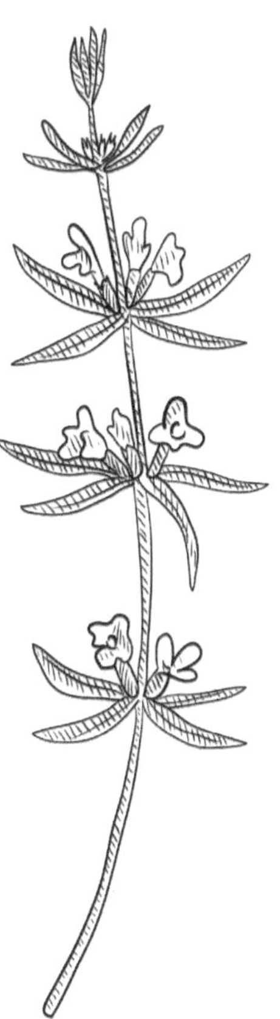

The English word "Savoury" probably derives from an old German name "Savaric "and this traveled to England with the Bretons when William of Normandy invaded England in 1066.

In Greece, Dioscuridis names the plant "thymbra" saying that the plant could be used in the same way as Thyme.

Nowadays savory means the opposite of sweet in common use and this herb can be described as spicy, even pungent so be warned not to add lots to any dish without tasting it first.

Healing Properties and Ancient and Modern Medicinal Use

Summer Savory (*Satureja hortensis*) is best grown as an annual but Winter Savory (*Satureja montana*) is a perennial herb up to USDA zone 6.

1. Winter Savory has been used to treat insect bites and stings by making a poultice with leaves directly on the affected area. If you have essential oil, you can use this directly on the skin as it is antifungal and antiseptic.
2. It can be used in hypothermia to bring its warming action to the person. Make a hot infusion of leaves.
3. It has also been used internally for nausea and indigestion by making an infusion of the leaves or eaten in food.
4. Winter savory gives some relief for menstrual pain too, taken as an infusion.
5. It is famous for the Dionysus legend and it is used as an aphrodisiac and also as a natural remedy for premature ejaculation.

Winter Gardening & how to Grow Winter Savory Inside

Winter Savory is happy outside, as its name suggests. My plants have survived frost, and rain and even poked their heads out of a covering of a foot of snow! This plant

grows wild in Crete on coastal, rocky mountainsides, and this gives you an idea of its ideal location.

It is a Mediterranean favorite and can be found from France through to Italy and Spain and in suitable soils all over Europe.

1. *Space*. It can grow up to 35 cm or slightly more so make sure you choose a sunny space and that it has room to spread.
2. *Soil* needs to have good drainage, and only water when there has been no rain for a long period.
3. *Indoors*. The plant may not thrive indoors because our heated homes are not the climate it prefers. Cuttings from the parent plant will be fine indoors and you can move them outside when the roots have settled.
4. You can keep picking all winter. This plant will survive almost anything.

Recipes, Tricks & Tips Using Winter Savory

This hardy plant can be moved indoors if snow is predicted, but in my experience, this plant survives the harshest of winters. Make sure the plant is located close to the back door, though, to avoid having to wear snow boots.

It's a robust -- some say spicy -- flavor, so don't treat it like basil or salad herbs. Use it sparingly as its leaves pack a punch. It's at its best when you allow it to cook through a dish, so the quiche below does it justice.

Winter Savory Quiche

There are a lot of eggs in this recipe, and the delicate taste of winter savory gives this quiche an unusual, festive flavor.

Serves: 6
Prep time: filling 30 minutes, base 15 minutes
Cook time: 30-40 minutes

Ingredients

- 2 Tbsp olive oil
- 3 onions
- 5 sprigs of winter savory
- ½ tsp freshly ground nutmeg
- Pinch of salt and black pepper
- 3 eggs
- 2 egg yolks
- ½ cup (125 ml) milk

- 1 cup (250 ml) cream
- 3.5 oz/100g cheese of your choice, grated

Method

1. Use the pastry base recipe in cinnamon to make a pastry base for the quiche.
2. Pre-bake the quiche base so it's ready for the filling when you start.
3. Set the oven to 375°F (190°C) to heat up.
4. To make the filling, peel and chop the onions and fry them in a little olive oil in a saucepan. Once they look golden-colored, add salt, pepper, and ground nutmeg, and fry for another 3 minutes. Remove the pan from the heat.
5. In a bowl, mix the eggs and the extra egg yolks with 80 ml of milk and cream. If the mixture seems too thick, gradually add a little extra milk.
6. Only add the leaves of the winter savory. Removing them is a bit fiddly, but I prefer not to find stalks when I'm eating, so I always remove them before I start. The stalks are edible, so this depends on you. Save a few leaves to add some to the top of the quiche.
7. Fill the empty quiche base by first adding the onions, followed by the egg mixture.
8. Top the quiche with the grated cheese and the remaining winter savory leaves.
9. Cook for 30 minutes. The eggs should cook to almost solid, and the cheese should look toasted.
10. Give each person a quarter of the quiche and serve with a fresh salad.

Conclusion

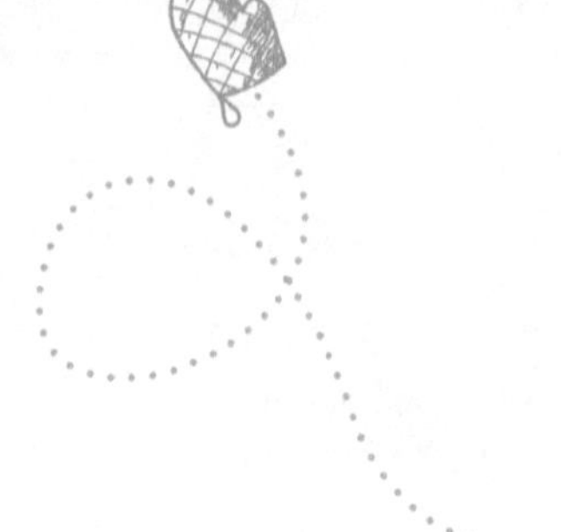

From our historical past to present-day living, this book deserves its spot on your bookshelf as a handy reference to 8 spices you can store and 10 herbs that will thrive in winter as well as in other seasons.

This book is your resource for warming recipes, as well as your chance to become an indoor herb gardener. By Christmas, your pots of herbs on that warm south-facing windowsill could be sprouting and you know that you can find recipes and tips for any winter emergency, like how to help a common cold with herbs. Know that humanity has acquired this knowledge over centuries, from as far back as the fifth century BCE, when the "Ice Maiden" in Siberia was buried with coriander seeds to right now, in your 21st-century living room and kitchen.

So enjoy a leaf of fresh sage as you water your plants, and add a leaf of tarragon or thyme, or ground spice to the soup you are making. Not only for the taste but also for the health benefits, these herbs and spices will make your culinary efforts even more worthwhile.

Resources and Useful Websites

Allspice

https://www.seedlipdrinks.com/en-us/
journal/a-brief-history-of-allspice/

https://www.simplyrecipes.com/what-is-allspice-and-how-i
s-it-used-5191895

https://www.seedlipdrinks.com/en-us/
journal/a-brief-history-of-allspice/

https://www.simplyrecipes.com/what-is-allspice-and-how-i
s-it-used-5191895

Basil

https://www.motherearthliving.com/health-and-wellness/
basil-herbal-lore-and-legends/

https://www.ncbi.nlm.nih.gov/pmc/articles/PMC6542390/

Biblical herbs

https://www.amazon.com/What-Bible-Says-Spices-Revealed/
dp/1506151337/ref

https://www.ourmidland.com/news/
article/Frawley-Many-herbs-we-use-toda
y-are-featured-in-7036751.php

Cardamom

https://www.myspicer.com/history-cardamom/

Cilantro

Cilantro: Health Benefits, Side Effects, Uses, Dose & Precautions (rxlist.com)

https://en.wikipedia.org/wiki/Pazyryk_burials

http://integrativemedicineofnj.com/cilantro-7-reasons-to-love-this-super-herb-for-your-health

Cloves

https://www.webmd.com/diet/health-benefits-cloves

https://www.mccormickscienceinstitute.com/resources/culinary-spices/herbs-spices/cloves

Ginger

https://www.ncbi.nlm.nih.gov/books/NBK92775/

Vimala, Norhanom, and Yadav 1999; Kapadia et al. 2002

Yagihashi, Miura, and Yagasaki 2008

Horseradish

Horseradish – Health Information Library | PeaceHealth

https://horseradish.org/horseradish-facts/horseradish-history/

https://www.botanical.com/botanical/mgmh/h/horrad38.html

Nutmeg

https://owlcation.com/humanities/The-Blood-Soaked-History-of-Nutmeg

Rosemary

https://www.gardensillustrated.com/news/rosemary-salvia-rhs-reclassified/

https://www.ncbi.nlm.nih.gov/pmc/articles/PMC4003706/

Star Anise

https://www.thespruceeats.com/what-is-star-anise-1328525

https://en.wikipedia.org/wiki/Illicium_verum

https://www.thespruceeats.com/what-is-star-anise-1328525

https://www.specialtyproduce.com/produce/Star_Anise_6144.php

Thyme

https://www.myspicer.com/the-history-of-thyme

https://www.ncbi.nlm.nih.gov/pmc/articles/PMC5483461

Winter herbs

https://theherbexchange.com/herbs-to-grow-in-winter-10-herbs-for-cold-season-harvests/

Winter Savory

https://www.wildherbsofcrete.com/winter-savory

https://en.wikipedia.org/wiki/Illicium_verum

Antioxidant & - inflammatory Properties of Herbs and Spices

https://www.nccih.nih.gov/health/antioxidants-in-depth

https://www.ncbi.nlm.nih.gov/pmc/articles/PMC5618098/

https://www.hsph.harvard.edu/nutritionsource/anti

https://www.goodreads.com/review/edit/63837458

Version v3 - 9.2025